Cooking Light

Diabetes

recipes • hints • tips

Feb. 2010

Oxmoor
House®

Welcome

If you're a busy home cook who has diabetes or cares for someone who does, then *Cooking Light Eat Smart Guide: Diabetes* is just what the doctor ordered! This digest-sized handbook is your indispensable diabetes-related resource for healthy shopping, quick cooking, and delicious eating.

Managing diabetes can be a daunting task, but *Cooking Light Eat Smart Guide: Diabetes* cuts through the clutter and gives you the tools to manage diabetes in a way that works for you. This handy go-to guide provides quick answers for those who are seeking specific, practical advice on how to make smart food choices.

If you or your loved ones are tired of eating the same things day after day, you'll be eager to try these 80 mouthwatering recipes ranging from quick-fix appetizers to decadent desserts. You'll also find too-good-to-be-true main dishes and sensational salads and side dishes that your whole family will enjoy. In addition, this throw-in-your purse guide offers at-a-glance information to make shopping and cooking faster, easier, and healthier than ever before.

Cooking Light Eat Smart Guide: Diabetes expedites your shopping and food preparation time and makes dinner a delicious experience once again. And coming from the most respected cooking authority in America—with more than 20 years of experience—we guarantee recipe satisfaction, expert nutritional analysis for each recipe, and sure-fire strategies for shopping faster, easier, and ultimately smarter every time.

Here's to your quest to eat smart, be fit, and live well,

The *Cooking Light* Editors

ISBN-13: 978-0-8487-3297-4
ISBN-10: 0-8487-3297-9
Library of Congress Control Number:
2009925690

Printed in the United States of America
First printing 2009

Be sure to check with your health-care provider
before making any changes in your diet.

OXMOOR HOUSE, INC.
VP, Publishing Director: Jim Childs
Editorial Director: Susan Payne Dobbs
Brand Manager: Allison Long Lowery
Managing Editor: L. Amanda Owens

Cooking Light® Eat Smart Guide: Diabetes

Editor: Heather Averett
Senior Designer: Emily Albright Parrish
Director, Test Kitchens: Elizabeth Tyler Austin
Assistant Director, Test Kitchens:
  Julie Christopher
Test Kitchens Professionals:
  Kathleen Royal Phillips,
  Catherine Crowell Steele,
  Ashley T. Strickland
Photography Director: Jim Bathie
Senior Photo Stylist: Kay E. Clarke
Associate Photo Stylist:
  Katherine Eckert Coyne
Production Manager: Theresa Beste-Farley

Contributors
Designer and Compositor: Carol O. Loria
Copy Editor: Rhonda Richards
Nutritional Analyses: Lauren Page;
  Kate Wheeler, R.D.
Interns: Emily Chappell, Georgia Dodge,
  Christine Taylor

To order additional publications,
call 1-800-765-6400

For more books to enrich your life,
visit **oxmoorhouse.com**

To search, savor, and share thousands
of recipes, visit **myrecipes.com**

Cooking Light®

Editor: Scott Mowbray
Executive Editor: Billy R. Sims
Managing Editor: Maelynn Cheung
Deputy Editor: Phillip Rhodes
Senior Food Editor: Ann Taylor Pittman
Projects Editor: Mary Simpson Creel, M.S., R.D.
Associate Food Editors: Timothy Q. Cebula;
  Kathy Kitchens Downie, R.D.;
  Julianna Grimes
Associate Editors: Cindy Hatcher,
  Brandy Rushing
Test Kitchen Director: Vanessa T. Pruett
Assistant Test Kitchen Director: Tiffany Vickers
Senior Food Stylist: Kellie Gerber Kelley
Test Kitchens Professionals:
  Mary Drennen Ankar, SaBrina Bone,
  Deb Wise
Art Director: Maya Metz Logue
Associate Art Directors:
  Fernande Bondarenko, J. Shay McNamee
Senior Designer: Brigette Mayer
Senior Photographer: Randy Mayor
Senior Photo Stylist: Cindy Barr
Photo Stylists: Jan Gautro, Leigh Ann Ross
Copy Chief: Maria Parker Hopkins
Assistant Copy Chief: Susan Roberts
Copy Editor: Johannah Gilman Paiva
Copy Researcher: Michelle Gibson Daniels
Production Manager: Liz Rhoades
Production Editor: Hazel R. Eddins
Cookinglight.com Editor: Kim Cross
Administrative Coordinator: Carol D. Johnson
Editorial Assistant: Jason Horn
Intern: Cassandra Blohowiak

Contents

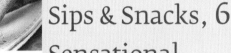

Sips & Snacks

QUICK&**EASY**

Rosemary Lemonade

  5 cups water
1½ cups fresh lemon juice (about
    10 large lemons)
  1 tablespoon minced fresh
    rosemary

½ cup "measures-like-sugar"
    calorie-free sweetener
Fresh rosemary sprigs (optional)

1. Combine water and lemon juice in a large nonaluminum saucepan; bring to a boil.

2. Remove from heat. Add rosemary; let stand 10 minutes. Strain mixture, discarding rosemary. Stir in sugar substitute. Cover and chill. Serve over ice. Garnish with fresh rosemary sprigs, if desired. **YIELD:** 6 servings (serving size: 1 cup).

CALORIES 16; FAT 0g; PROTEIN 0.2g; CARB 5.3g; FIBER 0.3g; CHOL 0mg; IRON 0mg; SODIUM 1mg; CALC 5mg

RECIPE BENEFITS: low-fat; low-sodium; low-carb

QUICK&**EASY**

Orange-Pineapple Slush

  3 cups ice cubes
  1 cup orange juice
½ cup pineapple juice

¼ cup lemon juice
3 tablespoons "measures-like-
    sugar" calorie-free sweetener

1. Combine all ingredients in a blender or food processor; process on high speed until smooth and frothy. Serve immediately. **YIELD:** 4 servings (serving size: 1 cup).

CALORIES 48; FAT 0.2g; PROTEIN 0.6g; CARB 11.8g; FIBER 0.3g; CHOL 0mg; IRON 0mg; SODIUM 1mg; CALC 12mg

RECIPE BENEFITS: low-fat; low-sodium; low-carb

Sparkling Peach Coolers

For nonalcoholic versions of both coolers, use 1 cup sugar-free
lemon-lime soft drink instead of the Champagne.

2 cups frozen sliced peaches, thawed	1 cup champagne, chilled
1 cup apricot nectar	½ cup club soda, chilled

1. Combine peaches and apricot nectar in container of an electric
blender; cover and process until smooth, stopping once to scrape
down sides. Pour into a pitcher.

2. Stir Champagne and club soda into peach mixture just before
serving. **YIELD:** 4 servings (serving size: 1 cup).

CALORIES 111; FAT 0.1g; PROTEIN 0.9g; CARB 18.7g; FIBER 1.7g; CHOL 0mg; IRON 0.5mg; SODIUM 8mg; CALC 6mg

RECIPE BENEFITS: low-fat; low-sodium

Strawberry Coolers

2½ cups fresh or frozen strawberries, thawed	1 cup Champagne, chilled
1 cup unsweetened orange juice	½ cup club soda, chilled

1. Combine strawberries and orange juice in container of an electric blender; top with cover, and process until smooth, stopping
once to scrape down sides. Pour into a pitcher.

2. Stir champagne and club soda into peach mixture just before
serving. **YIELD:** 4 servings (serving size: 1 cup).

CALORIES 103; FAT 0.1g; PROTEIN 1.2g; CARB 16.1g; FIBER 3.0g; CHOL 0mg; IRON 0.7mg; SODIUM 7mg; CALC 23mg

RECIPE BENEFITS: low-fat; low-sodium

take two:

Iced Tea vs.

Lemonade

It's a toss-up, nutritionally speaking, between the greater of two goods with these refreshing beverages.
Need a dose of vitamin C? A glass of lemonade contains between 15 and 20 percent of the recommended daily value. Freshly brewed tea contains no vitamin C but is a refreshing source of antioxidants. Normal blends contain polyphenols, antioxidants that may reduce cancer risk, and flavonoid-rich green and black teas raise the antioxidant power even more. Just watch the amount of added sugar to control the number of calories.

Black Currant-and-Raspberry Cooler

The fruited ice cubes add an elegant and tasty touch to this beverage—and they're so easy to make.

4½ cups cranberry-raspberry fruit juice blend, divided	14 mint leaves
14 raspberries	4½ cups water
	4 black currant-flavored tea bags

1. Pour 1 cup fruit juice into an ice cube tray; place 1 raspberry and 1 mint leaf in each section of ice cube tray. Freeze until firm.

2. Bring water to a boil in a medium saucepan. Add tea bags; remove from heat. Cover and steep 10 minutes. Remove and discard tea bags.

3. Combine tea and 3½ cups fruit juice in a large pitcher. Cover and chill. Place frozen juice cubes in glasses; pour tea mixture over cubes. **YIELD:** 6 servings (serving size: 1 cup).

CALORIES 126; FAT 0g; PROTEIN 0.2g; CARB 32g; FIBER 0.5g; CHOL 0mg; IRON 0.2mg; SODIUM 4mg; CALC 14mg

RECIPE BENEFITS: low-fat; low-sodium

Label Reading

Here are some things to consider when you use food labels to select items for your diabetic eating plan.

SERVING SIZE: Values are for one serving of food. A portion may be more or less than what you expect, so pay attention to the amount given.

TOTAL CARBOHYDRATE: Total Carbohydrate is just that—the total amount of carbohydrate in one serving. This value doesn't indicate what specific type of carbohydrate the food contains, simply a total amount.

DIETARY FIBER: Fiber is a type of carbohydrate, so even though it's listed separately, the value is included in the amount of Total Carbohydrate. In some carbohydrate-counting plans, you are instructed to subtract the grams of Dietary Fiber from the Total Carbohydrate to get the "net carbohydrate" that is actually absorbed.

SUGARS: The value for sugars is also part of the amount of Total Carbohydrate. This value refers to both natural sugars and added sugars. You cannot tell from this value what types of sugars are in the food, only the amount of sugars. It may be one type of sugar, or it may be a mix of sugars, but you need to look on the ingredients list panel to determine the types of sugar. The value for sugars gives part of the picture, but the main number to look at is the Total Carbohydrate.

Nutrition Facts

Serving Size 2 Cookies (24g)
Servings Per Container about 6

Amount Per Serving

Calories 110	Calories from Fat 60

	% Daily Value*
Total Fat 6g	**10%**
Saturated Fat 4g	**19%**
Polyunsaturated Fat 0g	
Monounsaturated Fat 1g	
Cholesterol 0mg	**0%**
Sodium 80mg	**3%**
Total Carbohydrate 16g	**5%**
Dietary Fiber 1g	**4%**
Sugars 0g	
Sugar Alcohol 6g	
Protein 1g	

Vitamin A 0% • Vitamin C 0% • Calcium 0% • Iron 4%

*Percent Daily Values are based on a 2,000 calorie diet. Your daily values may be higher or lower depending on your calorie needs:

	Calories:	2,000	2,500
Total Fat	Less than	65g	80g
Sat Fat	Less than	20g	25g
Cholesterol	Less than	300mg	300mg
Sodium	Less than	2,400mg	2,400mg
Total Carbohydrate		300g	375g
Dietary Fiber		25g	30g

g=grams mg=milligrams

SUGAR ALCOHOL: Some foods contain sweeteners in the form of sugar alcohols such as sorbitol, mannitol, and xylitol. You won't see the specific name of the sugar alcohol listed on the Nutrition Facts panel; they're listed generally as Sugar Alcohol.

Some product package labels display "Net Carb," which is usually the Total Carbohydrate minus the Sugar Alcohol. "Net Carb," however, is not an approved FDA label term, so it does not have an approved definition.

QUICK&EASY

Chilled Tomato Cocktail

Here's a spicy spin on a classic tomato cocktail. Every sip will have you smiling.

- 4 **cups no-salt-added tomato juice**
- 1 **teaspoon low-sodium Worcestershire sauce**
- ½ **teaspoon coarsely ground pepper**
- ½ **teaspoon prepared horseradish**
- 2 **cups club soda, chilled**
- **Lemon slices (optional)**
- **Green onions (optional)**

1. Combine first 4 ingredients in a large pitcher; stir well. Cover and chill.

2. Gently stir club soda into juice mixture just before serving. Serve over ice. If desired, garnish with lemon slices and green onions. **YIELD:** 6 servings (serving size: 1 cup).

CALORIES 29; FAT 0.1g; PROTEIN 1.3g; CARB 7.1g; FIBER 0.7g; CHOL 0mg; IRON 1mg; SODIUM 35mg; CALC 21mg

RECIPE BENEFITS: low-fat; low-sodium; low-carb

QUICK&EASY

Frosted Cappuccino

2 cups brewed espresso (or very strong brewed coffee), chilled
2 cups vanilla no-added-sugar, fat-free ice cream
½ teaspoon vanilla extract
Ground cinnamon (optional)

1. Combine first 3 ingredients in a blender; process until smooth. Pour into glasses. Sprinkle each serving with cinnamon, if desired. Serve immediately. **YIELD:** 4 servings (serving size: 1 cup).

CALORIES 94; FAT 0.2g (sat 0.1g, mono 0.0g, poly 0.1g); PROTEIN 3.1g; CARB 20.1g; FIBER 0g; CHOL 0mg; IRON 0mg; SODIUM 67mg; CALC 82mg

RECIPE BENEFITS: low-fat; low-sodium

QUICK&EASY

Sugar-Free Cocoa Mix

2⅓ cups instant nonfat dry milk
⅓ cup unsweetened cocoa
⅓ cup "measures-like-sugar" calorie-free sweetener
Miniature marshmallows (optional)
Sugar-free candy canes (optional)

1. Combine first 3 ingredients in a large bowl; stir well. Store in an airtight container.
2. To serve, spoon ¼ cup cocoa mix into each mug. Add 1 cup boiling water, and stir well. Top with miniature marshmallows or sugar-free candy canes, if desired (marshmallows and candy canes not included in analysis). **YIELD:** 12 servings (serving size: 1 cup).

CALORIES 53; FAT 0.3g (sat 0.2g, mono 0.1g, poly 0g); PROTEIN 5.2g; CARB 8.4g; FIBER 0.8g; CHOL 2mg; IRON 0mg; SODIUM 74mg; CALC 180mg

RECIPE BENEFITS: low-fat; low-sodium; low-carb

Cinnamon for Diabetes

Research has found that as little as 1 gram of cinnamon—less than half a teaspoon, or three calories' worth—has significant benefits for people with type II diabetes. In a study done at the Beltsville Human Nutrition Research Center in Maryland, 60 diabetics took a daily cinnamon capsule for 40 days and saw marked decreases in cholesterol and blood sugar levels after just 20 days. Researchers have found that compounds in cinnamon help make insulin more efficient, improving the hormone's ability to regulate glucose entry cells. To get your dose of cinnamon, there's no need to take supplements. You can cook with it, bake with it, or steep it in liquid, and you'll still get the benefits. Put it in coffee grounds, or steep a cinnamon stick in tea.

QUICK&**EASY**

Holiday Tea Mix

Warm up holiday guests with a mug of good cheer.
This tea mix also makes a great gift for friends and family.

- 1¼ cups "measures-like-sugar" calorie-free sweetener
- 1 (1.8-ounce) container sugar-free orange drink mix (such as sugar-free Tang)
- 1 (0.45-ounce) package sugar-free lemonade mix
- ¾ cup unsweetened instant tea without lemon
- 1 teaspoon ground cloves
- 2 teaspoons ground cinnamon

1. Combine all ingredients in a large bowl; stir well. Store in an airtight container.

2. To serve, spoon 2 teaspoons tea mix into each cup. Add ¾ cup boiling water, and stir well. **YIELD:** 54 servings (serving size: ¾ cup).

CALORIES 4; FAT 0g; PROTEIN 0.1g; CARB 0.4g; FIBER 0.1g; CHOL 0mg; IRON 0mg; SODIUM 5mg; CALC 78mg

RECIPE BENEFITS: low-fat; low-sodium; low-carb

Mulled Cider Supreme

A steaming fragrant mug of this cider is a welcome treat on a brisk fall afternoon. Garnish with a cinnamon stick or lemon slice, if desired.

4½ cups apple cider
1 cup water
2 tablespoons "measures-like-sugar" brown sugar calorie-free sweetener (such as Brown Sugar Twin)

2 (3-inch) cinnamon sticks
5 whole cloves
3 whole allspice
1 (2-inch) piece peeled fresh ginger

1. Combine first 3 ingredients in a saucepan, stirring well.
2. Place cinnamon sticks and remaining 3 ingredients on a 6-inch square of cheesecloth; tie with string. Add spice bag to cider mixture.
3. Bring to a simmer over medium-high heat, stirring occasionally. Reduce heat to low, and cook, uncovered, 15 minutes, stirring occasionally. Discard spice bag. Pour into individual mugs, and serve warm. **YIELD:** 5 servings (serving size: 1 cup).

CALORIES 128; FAT 0g; PROTEIN 1g; CARB 32g; FIBER 0g; CHOL 0mg; IRON 0mg; SODIUM 3mg; CALC 5mg

RECIPE BENEFITS: low-fat; low-sodium

QUICK&**EASY**

Hot Cranberry Cocktail

Reduce your party-planning stress with this festive beverage that has only 4 ingredients and takes less than 10 minutes to prepare.

1 tablespoon whole cloves
2 teaspoons whole allspice
4 cups pineapple juice

1 (48-ounce) bottle low-calorie cranberry juice drink

1. Cut a 6-inch square of cheesecloth; place cloves and allspice in center, and tie with string.
2. Combine spice bag, pineapple juice, and cranberry juice in a large saucepan. Bring to a boil; cover, reduce heat, and simmer 5 minutes. Remove and discard spice bag. Serve warm. YIELD: 10 servings (serving size: 1 cup).

CALORIES 80; FAT 0.1g; PROTEIN 0.3g; CARB 20g; FIBER 0.1g; CHOL 0mg; IRON 0mg; SODIUM 46mg; CALC 0mg

RECIPE BENEFITS: low-fat; low-sodium

> **QUICK TIP:** Combine one part nutmeg with two parts each cinnamon and cloves to make your own allspice substitute if you don't have any allspice on hand.

CHOICE INGREDIENT: *Allspice Berry*

Named for a taste combination that includes cinnamon, nutmeg, cloves, and black pepper, allspice is the pea-sized berry of an evergreen pimento tree. Peppercorn-like in appearance, this dark, reddish-brown spice has a mildly sweet flavor and a variety of uses. Both whole or ground allspice berry can be used to season sauces, relishes, and preserves; add flavor to meats and stews; and give a hint of spice to baked goods. It's also a key ingredient in jerk seasoning and provides a pungent, spicy taste to teas and ciders.

Party On!

Don't let the temptation of party goodies wreck your diabetes control. Here's how to steer smoothly through any gathering.

Treats offered at holiday parties and special family celebrations may be tempting, but they can wreak havoc with blood sugars. Here are some tricks for sticking to diet plans during social occasions.

- Eat a regular meal before you go to a party. Then you won't be hungry and tempted to overindulge in snacks and sweets.

- Don't skip meals during the day to "save up" for overeating at the party.

- Keep a glass of water or sugar-free soft drink in your hand at all times. It's harder to eat when one hand is busy.

- Don't stand next to the serving table all night. Move to another place in the room.

- Enjoy conversation. When your mouth is busy talking, it's not busy eating.

- Drink lots of water before a party. You'll feel full and be less tempted to snack.

- Offer to bring a low-fat, low-sugar dish to the party.

- Fill up on low-calorie, high-fiber foods, such as fresh vegetables and fruits. But go easy on the vegetable dip and cheese.

- If you must have something sweet, go ahead and have a little taste. Just allow for the extra carbohydrate in your meal plan.

- Keep the fat content of your regular meals especially low during the holidays to balance the extra fat from party foods.

- Share ideas for healthful treats as a holiday gift to your friends. Furnish them with healthy recipes as they plan holiday parties. Or go a step further and put together a booklet of healthy (and diabetes-friendly) recipes.

Party Picks

CHOOSE THESE LOW-FAT, LOW-SUGAR PARTY FOODS.

FRUITS
Apple wedges
Grapes
Pear slices
Pineapple
Strawberries

VEGETABLES
Broccoli florets
Carrot sticks
Cauliflower
Celery sticks
Cherry tomatoes
Squash slices

BREADS & STARCHES
Breadsticks
French bread
Low-fat potato chips
Low-fat tortilla chips
Melba rounds
Pita bread wedges
Plain crackers
Plain rolls
Pretzels

MEATS, POULTRY & SEAFOOD
Lean roast beef
Pork tenderloin
Turkey
Boiled shrimp

DIPS
Black bean dip
Salsa

Lightly spiced with cinnamon and nutmeg, these sweetened nuts can be eaten as a crunchy snack or used as a topping for low-sugar ice cream.

Spiced Pecans

½ cup "measures-like-sugar" calorie-free sweetener
1½ teaspoons ground cinnamon
1 teaspoon ground nutmeg
¼ teaspoon salt
1 large egg white
4½ teaspoons water
2½ cups pecan halves
Cooking spray

1. Preheat oven to 300°.

2. Combine first 4 ingredients in a medium bowl, stirring well.

3. Beat egg white and water with a mixer at medium speed until foamy. Gradually add sweetener mixture, 1 tablespoon at a time, beating until stiff peaks form; fold in pecan halves.

4. Pour pecan mixture onto a jelly-roll pan coated with cooking spray. Bake at 300° for 25 minutes, stirring every 10 minutes.

5. Cool completely in pan. Store in an airtight container. YIELD: 20 servings (serving size: 2 tablespoons).

CALORIES 100; FAT 9.7g (sat 0.9g, mono 0.0g, poly 0.0g); PROTEIN 1.5g; CARB 2.6g; FIBER 0.9g; CHOL 0mg; IRON 0.3mg; SODIUM 32mg; CALC 2mg

RECIPE BENEFITS: low-sodium; low-carb

> **NUTRITION TIP:** Nuts are jam-packed with micronutrients such as vitamin E, folic acid, niacin, copper, magnesium, and potassium. They're also rich in arginine, which the body uses to make a potent natural vasodilator. And don't forget the abundant flavonoids and isoflavones—the most recently discovered "guardian angel" compounds now thought to help ward off cancer and cardiovascular disease.

Crisp and Spicy Snack Mix

Not your average snack mix, this one is bursting with flavor from ginger stir-fry sauce, chili powder, and cumin.

2 cups crisscross of corn and rice cereal (such as Crispix)
1 cup tiny pretzel twists
½ cup reduced-fat wheat crackers (such as Wheat Thins)
½ cup reduced-fat cheddar crackers (such as Cheez-It)

1½ tablespoons butter, melted
1 tablespoon ginger stir-fry sauce (such as Lawry's)
1 teaspoon chili powder
1 teaspoon ground cumin
¼ teaspoon salt
Cooking spray

1. Preheat oven to 250°.

2. Combine first 4 ingredients in a bowl. Combine butter, stir-fry sauce, chili powder, cumin, and salt; drizzle over cereal mixture, tossing to coat. Spread mixture into a jelly roll pan coated with cooking spray. Bake at 250° for 30 minutes or until crisp, stirring twice. **YIELD:** 4 cups (serving size: ½ cup).

CALORIES 117; FAT 3.9g (sat 1.7g, mono 0.7g, poly 0.5g); PROTEIN 2.2g; CARB 18.5g; FIBER 0.8g; CHOL 6mg; IRON 2.6mg; SODIUM 368mg; CALC 17mg

CHOICE INGREDIENT: *Basil*

Basil is one of the most important culinary herbs. Sweet basil, the most common type, is redolent of licorice and cloves. Basil is used in the south of France to make *pistou;* its Italian cousin, pesto, is made just over the border. Used in sauces, sandwiches, soups, and salads, basil is in top form when married to tomatoes.

Herbed Goat Cheese

This is a simple make-ahead recipe, ideal for entertaining.

⅓ cup chopped fresh basil

1 teaspoon grated lemon rind

2 tablespoons fresh lemon juice

1 tablespoon extra-virgin olive oil

2 teaspoons chopped fresh oregano

¼ teaspoon salt

¼ teaspoon freshly ground black pepper

2 garlic cloves, minced

1 (3-ounce) package goat cheese

1 (8-ounce) French baguette, cut into 16 slices, toasted

1. Combine first 8 ingredients in a small bowl, stirring well. Coat cheese evenly with basil mixture, pressing gently to adhere. Cover and refrigerate at least 2 hours. Serve cheese with baguette slices. **YIELD:** 8 servings (serving size: ¾ ounce cheese and 2 bread slices).

CALORIES 122; FAT 4g (sat 1.8g, mono 1.9g, poly 0.2g); PROTEIN 4.6g; CARB 17.8g; FIBER 0.6g; CHOL 5mg; IRON 1.2mg; SODIUM 296mg; CALC 21mg

> **FLAVOR TIP:** The longer the cheese refrigerates, the more flavor it absorbs from the herbs. You can leave it to marinate for up to two days. For optimal flavor, let the goat cheese stand at room temperature about 10 minutes before serving.

Parmesan-Coated Brie

1 large egg, lightly beaten
1 tablespoon water
¼ cup dry breadcrumbs
¼ cup grated fat-free Parmesan
   cheese

1½ teaspoons dried Italian seasoning
1 (15-ounce) round Brie cheese
   with herbs
Cooking spray
Fresh rosemary sprigs (optional)

1. Combine egg and water in a shallow dish. Combine breadcrumbs, Parmesan cheese, and seasoning in another shallow dish.

2. Dip Brie into egg mixture, turning to coat top and sides (do not

coat bottom). Place Brie in breadcrumb mixture, turning to coat top and sides. Repeat procedure. Place on a baking sheet coated with cooking spray. Chill at least 1 hour.

3. Preheat oven to 375°.

4. Bake at 375° for 10 minutes. Garnish with rosemary, if desired. Serve with low-fat crackers or French baguette slices (crackers and bread not included in analysis). **Yield:** 15 appetizer servings.

CALORIES 113; FAT 8.4g (sat 5.1g, mono 2.4g, poly 0.3g); PROTEIN 7.3g; CARB 2.2g; FIBER 0.1g; CHOL 43mg; IRON 0mg; SODIUM 217mg; CALC 68mg

RECIPE BENEFITS: low-carb

QUICK&EASY

Light Guacamole

- 1 large Anaheim chile (about 3 ounces)
- 2 green onions, cut into 2-inch pieces
- 2 garlic cloves, peeled and halved
- 2 large plum tomatoes, quartered
- ¾ cup peeled diced avocado (about 1 small)
- ½ cup tomatillo salsa
- ¼ cup cilantro sprigs
- 2 tablespoons fresh lemon or lime juice
- ½ teaspoon ground cumin
- ¼ teaspoon salt
- Lime slices (optional)

1. Cut chile in half lengthwise; discard stem, seeds, and membranes.
2. Place chile, green onions, and garlic in a food processor; pulse 5 times or until coarsely chopped. Add tomato and next 6 ingredients; pulse 10 times until blended (mixture should be chunky). Spoon into a bowl; garnish with lime slices, if desired. Serve with low-fat tortilla chips (chips not included in analysis). **YIELD:** 2 cups (serving size: ¼ cup).

CALORIES 57; FAT 4g (sat 5.6g, mono 2.4g, poly 0.5g); PROTEIN 1g; CARB 5.5g; FIBER 1.8g; CHOL 0mg; IRON 0.6mg; SODIUM 126mg; CALC 11mg

RECIPE BENEFITS: low-sodium; low-carb

KITCHEN HOW TO
Prepare Avocados

Avocados contain heart-healthy, monounsaturated fat and are loaded with antioxidants and potassium (more per serving than bananas). Add their buttery texture and mild, nutty flavor to sandwiches and salads, in addition to guacamole. To easily dice, start with an 8- to 10-inch chef's knife. Insert it into the top where the stem was (it will be a darker area), and gently press down until you reach the pit. Then follow the tips below.

1. With the knife steady, rotate the fruit so the knife travels around the pit, cutting the entire avocado.

2. Remove the knife, then slowly and gently twist the two sides away from each other to separate.

3. Strike the pit, and pierce it with the blade. Then twist and remove the knife; the pit will come with it.

4. Use the knife's tip to pierce the flesh in horizontal and vertical rows. Be careful not to cut through the skin.

5. Remove the meat gently with a spoon. To prevent browning, squeeze lemon juice on the flesh.

❶

❷

❸

❹

❺

Hot Artichoke Cheese Dip

- 2 garlic cloves
- 1 green onion, cut into pieces
- ⅓ cup (1½ ounces) grated Parmigiano-Reggiano cheese, divided
- ⅓ cup reduced-fat mayonnaise
- ¼ cup (2 ounces) ⅓-less-fat cream cheese
- 1 tablespoon fresh lemon juice
- ¼ teaspoon crushed red pepper
- 12 ounces frozen artichoke hearts, thawed and drained
- Cooking spray
- 24 (½-ounce) slices baguette, toasted

1. Preheat oven to 400°.

2. Place garlic and onion in a food processor; process until finely chopped. Add ¼ cup Parmigiano-Reggiano and next 4 ingredients; process until almost smooth. Add artichoke hearts; pulse until artichoke hearts are coarsely chopped. Spoon mixture into a 3-cup gratin dish coated with cooking spray; sprinkle evenly with remaining Parmigiano-Reggiano. Bake at 400° for 15 minutes or until thoroughly heated and bubbly. Serve hot with baguette. **YIELD:** 12 servings (serving size: 2½ tablespoons dip and 2 baguette slices).

CALORIES 126; FAT 3.4g (sat 1.3g, mono 0.6g, poly 0.5g); PROTEIN 5.1g; CARB 20.8g; FIBER 2.3g; CHOL 7mg; IRON 1.1mg; SODIUM 334mg; CALC 59mg

Creamy Feta-Spinach Dip

This version of spinach dip is made tangier with the addition of feta cheese and low-fat yogurt. With only 1.4 grams of fat and less than 1 gram of carbohydrate per tablespoon, you can afford to splurge on a couple of extra servings. But don't forget to count the carbs in the bread or crackers—they're not included in the analysis.

1 (8-ounce) carton plain low-fat yogurt
¾ cup (3 ounces) crumbled feta cheese
¼ cup (2 ounces) ⅓-less-fat cream cheese, softened
¼ cup low-fat sour cream
1 garlic clove, crushed
1½ cups finely chopped spinach
1 tablespoon minced fresh or 1 teaspoon dried dill
⅛ teaspoon black pepper
Fresh dill (optional)

1. Spoon yogurt onto several layers of heavy-duty paper towels; spread to ½-inch thickness. Cover with additional paper towels, and let stand 5 minutes.

2. Scrape yogurt into the bowl of a food processor using a rubber spatula. Add the cheeses, sour cream, and garlic, and process until smooth, scraping sides of bowl once.

3. Spoon yogurt mixture into a medium bowl, and stir in the spinach, minced dill, and pepper. Cover and chill. Garnish with fresh dill, if desired. **YIELD:** 2 cups (serving size: ¼ cup).

CALORIES 78; FAT 5.4g (sat 3.4g, mono 1.4g, poly 0.2g); PROTEIN 4.2g; CARB 3.6g; FIBER 0.4g; CHOL 20mg; IRON 0.4mg; SODIUM 178mg; CALC 130mg

RECIPE BENEFITS: low-carb

Hot Crab Dip

Serve warm with toasted pita chips or melba toast.

1 cup fat-free cottage cheese
½ teaspoon grated lemon rind
2 tablespoons lemon juice
1 tablespoon Dijon mustard
1½ teaspoons Worcestershire sauce
1 teaspoon hot sauce
½ teaspoon salt
⅛ teaspoon freshly ground black pepper
1 garlic clove, minced
1 (8-ounce) block ⅓-less-fat cream cheese, softened
2 tablespoons chopped green onion
1 pound lump crabmeat, shell pieces removed
Cooking spray
2 tablespoons grated fresh Parmesan cheese
¼ cup dry breadcrumbs

1. Preheat oven to 375°.

2. Combine first 9 ingredients in a food processor; process until smooth.

3. Combine cottage cheese mixture, cream cheese, and onion in a large bowl; gently fold in crab. Place crab mixture in an 11 x 7-inch baking dish coated with cooking spray. Bake at 375° for 30 minutes. Sprinkle with Parmesan and breadcrumbs. Bake at 375° for 15 minutes or until lightly golden. **YIELD:** 20 servings (serving size: about 3 tablespoons).

CALORIES 63; FAT 3.1g (sat 1.8g, mono 0.1g, poly 0g); PROTEIN 6.8g; CARB 1.9g; FIBER 0.1g; CHOL 30mg; IRON 0.3mg; SODIUM 264mg; CALC 29mg

RECIPE BENEFITS: low-carb

INGREDIENT TIP: Even though the meat that you pull from the shell has the best flavor, you can also buy delicious crabmeat that is freshly cooked, unpasteurized, and packed in plastic tubs. Lump crabmeat (also called backfin or jumbo) is the most desirable.

Focus on Fun

Keeping your blood sugars in control during the holidays can be a challenge. But if you find ways to take some of the focus away from food, you're in for great success. Here are some suggestions for other party activities besides eating:

- Sing carols around the piano.

- Go caroling in the neighborhood.

- Ask any musicians in the group to bring their instruments, and invite them to play.

- Exchange gag gifts.

- Share stories of holiday memories.

- Address cards to nursing home residents, hospital patients, or members of the armed services.

- Wrap toys for needy children.

- Collect canned goods for a local food bank.

- Play charades or any group game.

- Watch a holiday classic movie.

Holiday Hospitality Tips

WHETHER YOU HAVE DIABETES, OR YOU'RE ENTERTAINING FOR PEOPLE WHO DO, HERE ARE SOME TIPS THAT WILL MAKE YOU A GREAT HOST.

• Have plenty of sugar-free drinks available.

• Make a special sugar-free dessert or purchase a carton of no-sugar-added ice cream.

• Let guests know which dishes do not have sugar if it's not obvious.

• Include a fresh vegetable tray or fruit and cheese platter on your menu.

• If you're serving dinner, let guests know what time you plan to serve so that those on insulin can plan when to take their injection.

• Serve flavored coffee with dessert. It's easier to pass up a high-sugar dessert if you have a sweet-tasting cup of coffee to savor.

• Have a place in the house other than the food table where people can gather.

Red Pepper Pesto Crostini

This red pepper pesto adds zest to grilled fish, pasta, or a sandwich.

1 (7-ounce) jar roasted red pepper, drained and coarsely chopped
3 tablespoons freshly grated Parmesan cheese
1 tablespoon sliced almonds, toasted
2 teaspoons no-salt-added tomato paste
1 garlic clove, chopped
3 ounces fat-free cream cheese
16 (½-inch-thick) slices French bread baguette, toasted

1. Combine first 5 ingredients in a blender; process until smooth, stopping once to scrape down sides. Cover and chill at least 1 hour.
2. Spread cream cheese evenly on toast slices; top each with 1 tablespoon pepper mixture. **Yield:** 16 appetizers.

CALORIES 44; FAT 0.6g (sat 0.3g, mono 0.1g, poly 0.1g); PROTEIN 2.4g; CARB 7.3g; FIBER 0.3g; CHOL 1mg; IRON 0.4mg; SODIUM 156mg; CALC 30mg

RECIPE BENEFITS: low-fat; low-carb

Mexican Pinwheels

No Super Bowl party is complete without these festive pinwheels. Wrap them up, and watch them go.

1 (8-ounce) package fat-free cream cheese, softened
½ cup fat-free sour cream
1 cup (4 ounces) shredded reduced-fat sharp Cheddar cheese
⅓ cup chopped green onions
¼ teaspoon salt-free herb-and-spice blend

1 (4.5-ounce) can chopped green chiles, drained
1 (2¼-ounce) can sliced ripe olives, drained
1 garlic clove, pressed
8 (8-inch) flour tortillas

1. Beat cream cheese and sour cream with a mixer at medium speed until smooth. Stir in Cheddar cheese and next 5 ingredients. Spread cheese mixture evenly over each tortilla; roll up tortillas. Wrap each separately in plastic wrap. Chill up to 8 hours.
2. To serve, unwrap each roll, and cut into 8 slices. Secure pinwheels with wooden picks, if desired. **YIELD:** 32 servings (serving size: 2 pinwheels).

CALORIES 56; FAT 1.3g (sat 0.7g, mono 0.2g, poly 0g); PROTEIN 3.3g; CARB 7.7g; FIBER 0.7g; CHOL 4mg; IRON 0.1mg; SODIUM 147mg; CALC 49mg

RECIPE BENEFITS: low-fat; low-carb

Pizza Bites

Not just tasty party pizzas, these little bites are also great for after-school snacking.

- ¾ cup (3 ounces) shredded part-skim mozzarella cheese
- ⅓ cup grated fresh Parmesan cheese
- 1 (14-ounce) package mini English muffins
- ⅓ cup chopped Canadian bacon
- ⅓ cup chopped green bell pepper

1. Preheat oven to 400°.

2. Combine mozzarella and Parmesan cheeses; set aside.

3. Cut each muffin in half horizontally and place on an ungreased baking sheet. Sprinkle bacon, green bell pepper, and cheese mixture evenly on muffin halves.

4. Bake at 400° for 10 to 12 minutes or until lightly browned. Serve warm. **YIELD:** 2 dozen (serving size: 1 appetizer).

CALORIES 57; FAT 1.4g (sat 0.7g, mono 0.3g, poly 0.2g); PROTEIN 3.1g; CARB 7.8g; FIBER 0g; CHOL 3mg; IRON 0.5mg; SODIUM 114mg; CALC 71mg

RECIPE BENEFITS: low-fat; low-sodium; low-carb

MAKE AHEAD

West Indies Shrimp

With only 2 grams of carbohydrate and less than 2 grams of fat per serving, what's not to love about this make-ahead party appetizer? You can cook the shrimp and make the marinade ahead. Combine them just before serving.

12 cups water	1 cup chopped green bell pepper
2 pounds unpeeled medium shrimp	2/3 cup cider vinegar
2 teaspoons Old Bay seasoning	1 1/2 tablespoons vegetable oil
1 cup chopped onion	1 teaspoon salt
	1/4 teaspoon black pepper

1. Bring water to a boil in a large saucepan. Add shrimp and seasoning; cook 3 minutes or until done. Drain and cool completely. Place shrimp in a large zip-top plastic bag. Add remaining ingredients; seal and marinate in refrigerator 30 minutes, turning

bag occasionally. Remove shrimp from bag, reserving marinade. Peel shrimp; place in a large bowl. Add reserved marinade; toss gently to coat. **YIELD:** 18 servings (serving size: about 2 shrimp).

CALORIES 57; FAT 1.8g (sat 0.3g, mono 0.4g, poly 0.8g); PROTEIN 7.9g; CARB 2.1g; FIBER 0.3g; CHOL 57mg; IRON 1.1mg; SODIUM 260mg; CALC 23mg

RECIPE BENEFITS: low-fat; low-carb

STORAGE TIP: Because most shrimp are quick-frozen at sea and then defrosted for sale, we often get asked if it's ok to refreeze them. We've done it for years without any problem so that we could store unused shrimp for later use. When you want to use your refrozen shrimp, just thaw them out in a bowl or sink filled with tap water.

Sensational Salads & Sides

Autumn Salad with Red Wine Vinaigrette

Eating five to eight servings of fruits and vegetables each day is part of a healthy diet. This salad helps put you on the right track to achieving success.

2 tablespoons extra-virgin olive oil
2 tablespoons red wine vinegar
$\frac{1}{2}$ teaspoon sugar
$\frac{1}{2}$ teaspoon minced garlic
$\frac{1}{4}$ teaspoon paprika
$\frac{1}{4}$ teaspoon dry mustard
$\frac{1}{8}$ teaspoon salt
Pinch of dried basil
Pinch of ground red pepper

5 cups mixed salad greens
4 cups torn romaine lettuce
$2\frac{1}{2}$ cups cubed Asian pear (about 1 large)
2 cups chopped Granny Smith apple (about 1 large)
$\frac{1}{2}$ cup thinly sliced red onion
$\frac{1}{4}$ cup (1 ounce) crumbled goat cheese

1. Combine first 9 ingredients in a bowl, stirring with a whisk.

2. Combine salad greens, romaine lettuce, Asian pear, apple, and red onion in a large bowl. Drizzle with vinaigrette, and toss well to coat.

3. Sprinkle with crumbled goat cheese. **YIELD:** 12 servings (serving size: about 1 cup salad and 1 teaspoon cheese).

CALORIES 48; FAT 3.2g (sat 0.8g, mono 2g, poly 0.3g); PROTEIN 1g; CARB 4.7g; FIBER 1.4g; CHOL 2mg; IRON 0.4mg; SODIUM 40mg; CALC 19mg

RECIPE BENEFITS: low-sodium; low-carb

Pineapple-Mango Salad

Be sure to wear plastic gloves when handling fresh jalapeños so that your skin won't get burned.

1 cup fresh pineapple chunks
¾ cup cubed peeled ripe mango (about 1)
¾ cup chopped red bell pepper (about 1)
1 orange
2 tablespoons finely chopped seeded jalapeño pepper (about 1)
1½ tablespoons sugar

1. Combine first 3 ingredients in a medium bowl; set aside.
2. Grate 1 teaspoon rind from orange. Peel orange, and cut out sections over a small bowl; squeeze membranes to extract juice. Reserve 2 tablespoons juice. Discard remaining juice and membranes. Add reserved orange rind and sections to mango mixture. Add jalapeño pepper, reserved orange juice, and sugar; toss gently. Let stand 10 minutes. **YIELD:** 5 servings (serving size: ½ cup).

CALORIES 54; FAT 0.2g (sat 0g, mono 0g, poly 0.1g); PROTEIN 0.9g; CARB 13.5g; FIBER 2.0g; CHOL 0mg; IRON 0.29mg; SODIUM 2mg; CALC 20mg

RECIPE BENEFITS: low-fat; low-sodium

Create a Diabetes-Friendly Kitchen

When you have the equipment and supplies you need on hand, healthy cooking becomes a way of life instead of a challenge. You don't need a lot of fancy gadgets and gourmet foods—just start with the basics.

Top 10 Healthy Cooking Tools

Quick and easy healthy cooking is no problem when you have the right tools. Here are the 10 items our food editors say they can't live without.

1. Set of sharp knives: Chopping fresh fruits and vegetables is quick and easy when you use sharp knives.

2. Microwave oven: Use for melting, steaming vegetables, toasting nuts, and defrosting, as well as a host of other "quick-fix" steps that will reduce your prep time.

3. Measuring spoons: Select a set of spoons that gradu-ate from ⅛ teaspoon to 1 tablespoon so you don't have to guess at amounts.

4. Dry and liquid measuring cups: Use the appropriate measuring cup, either dry or liquid, so your amounts will be accurate.

5. Nonstick skillets, saucepans, and baking pans: You don't have to use much fat, if any, when you cook or bake in nonstick pans. And cleanup is a breeze!

6. Food scales: Use a scale to make sure pieces of meat, poultry, and fish are the specified weight, or to measure the correct amount of cheese.

7. Kitchen scissors: Scissors are handy for mincing herbs, chopping tomatoes in the can, trimming fat from meats and poultry—plus many more uses.

8. Instant-read thermometer: A key safety factor is cooking food to the proper temperature, so use an instant-read thermometer to check eggs, meats, and poultry.

9. Steam basket or vegetable steamer: Steaming veg-gies is an easy, healthy way to cook vegetables, because it preserves nutrients as well as flavor.

10. Broiler pan/broiler pan rack: When you broil, much of the fat drips away into the pan, so broiling is a quick, low-fat cooking method.

Greek Salad Bowl

- 1 (14-ounce) can quartered artichoke hearts, drained
- 1 cup sliced cucumber
- ⅓ cup crumbled feta cheese
- 12 kalamata olives
- 1 large tomato, cut into thin wedges
- ⅓ cup fresh lemon juice
- 1 tablespoon olive oil
- ½ teaspoon dried oregano
- ½ teaspoon lemon pepper seasoning
- 1 garlic clove, crushed
- Freshly ground black pepper (optional)

1. Combine first 5 ingredients in a large bowl. Combine lemon juice and next 4 ingredients in a small bowl; stir with a whisk until blended. Pour over vegetable mixture; toss to coat. Sprinkle with pepper, if desired. **YIELD:** 6 (¾-cup) servings.

CALORIES 89; FAT 6.1g (sat 1.8g, mono 3.6g, poly 0.6g); PROTEIN 2.7g; CARB 6.3g; FIBER 2.5g; CHOL 7mg; IRON 0.9mg; SODIUM 358mg; CALC 54mg

RECIPE BENEFITS: low-carb

CHOICE INGREDIENT: *Kalamata olives*

One of the more popular varieties, these Greek black olives are plump and juicy with a powerful flavor, bright acidity, and high salt content. They are delicious with soy products such as tofu and tempeh and work wonders with leafy greens and cruciferous vegetables (such as broccoli and cauliflower) tempering bitterness with acidity.

Bean and Pasta Salad

8 ounces uncooked farfalle (bow tie pasta)	2 tablespoons chopped fresh cilantro
1 (15-ounce) can no-salt-added black beans, rinsed and drained	2 garlic cloves, minced
1 pint cherry tomatoes, halved	1 cup fat-free Italian dressing
1 green bell pepper, chopped	3 tablespoons grated fresh Parmesan cheese
1 large lime, cut in half	

1. Cook pasta according to package directions; omit salt and fat.

2. Place beans, tomatoes, and pepper in a large bowl. Squeeze lime juice over bean mixture; discard lime rind. Add cilantro and garlic to bean mixture.

3. Drain pasta; add to bean mixture. Pour dressing over salad, tossing gently to coat; sprinkle with cheese. Cover and chill at least 8 hours. **YIELD:** 6 servings (serving size: 1½ cups).

CALORIES 227; FAT 2.1g (sat 0.8g, mono 0.1g, poly 0.2g); PROTEIN 10.4g; CARB 42.7g; FIBER 4.7g; CHOL 3mg; IRON 2.4mg; SODIUM 495mg; CALC 99mg

RECIPE BENEFITS: low-fat

QUICK&**EASY**

Salad Niçoise

¼ **pound fresh green beans, trimmed**

3 **small red potatoes, sliced**

1 **(8-ounce) tuna steak (¾-inch thick)**

⅓ **cup white wine vinegar**

1½ **tablespoons lemon juice**

1½ **teaspoons Dijon mustard**

2 **cups torn Bibb lettuce or leaf lettuce**

1 **tomato, cut into 8 wedges**

¼ **teaspoon freshly ground black pepper**

1. Arrange green beans and potatoes on one side of a vegetable steamer over boiling water in a Dutch oven. Place tuna on opposite side of basket. Cover and steam 8 to 10 minutes or until fish flakes easily when tested with a fork. Set tuna aside to cool. Plunge beans and potatoes into ice water to cool.

2. Combine vinegar, lemon juice, and mustard in a jar; cover tightly, and shake vigorously.

3. Place lettuce on a serving platter. Drain potatoes and beans; arrange over lettuce. Flake tuna, and place on salad; add tomato wedges. Drizzle with vinegar mixture. Sprinkle with freshly ground pepper. **YIELD:** 2 servings.

CALORIES 349; FAT 1.7g (sat 0.4g, mono 0.2g, poly 0.6g); PROTEIN 33.6g; CARB 49.9g; FIBER 6.9g; CHOL 51mg; IRON 3.7mg; SODIUM 166mg; CALC 83mg

take two:
Wild Salmon vs. Yellowfin Tuna

You can't go wrong choosing between seasonal fresh fish like yellowfin tuna and wild salmon. Both contain the same number of calories, but yellowfin tuna (sometimes referred to as "ahi") is less fatty, offers eight more grams of protein than wild salmon, and is prized for its mild but not fishy flavor. Although wild salmon contains more fat, it also has more heart-healthy omega-3 fatty acids.

Yellowfin Tuna	**Wild Salmon**
(4½ ounces cooked)	(4½ ounces cooked)
177 calories	177 calories
1.6 grams total fat	5.5 grams total fat
0.35 grams omega-3s	1.35 grams omega-3s
38 grams protein	30 grams protein

Orange-Pecan Mixed Green Salad

For a richer, nuttier salad, toast the pecans in a skillet over medium heat for 5 minutes, stirring often.

¼ cup balsamic vinegar
¼ cup water
1 tablespoon minced onion
1 teaspoon olive oil
¾ teaspoon cornstarch

4 cups mixed salad greens
1 large navel orange, peeled and cut into 8 slices
2 tablespoons chopped pecans

1. Combine first 5 ingredients in a 2-cup glass measure; stir well. Microwave, uncovered, at HIGH 1 minute or until mixture boils and is slightly thickened. Stir until smooth. Let cool to room temperature.

2. Place 1 cup salad greens on each of 4 plates. Cut orange slices in half. Arrange slices over salad greens, and sprinkle with pecans. Drizzle evenly with vinaigrette. **YIELD:** 4 servings (serving size: 1 cup greens, 4 orange slices, ½ tablespoon pecans, and about 2 tablespoons vinaigrette).

CALORIES 77; FAT 4g (sat 0.4g, mono 2.4g, poly 1g); PROTEIN 1.6g; CARB 9.4g; FIBER 2.4g; CHOL 0mg; IRON 1mg; SODIUM 18mg; CALC 51mg

RECIPE BENEFITS: low-sodium; low-carb

| QUICK&EASY |

Spinach Salad with the Blues

If you're a true blue cheese lover, this salad will become one of your favorites.

⅓ cup fat-free, less-sodium chicken broth

¼ cup white wine vinegar

1 tablespoon prepared mustard

1 teaspoon "measures-like-sugar" calorie-free sweetener

1 (10-ounce) package torn fresh spinach

5 heads Belgian endive (about 10 ounces), washed and trimmed

2 Red Delicious apples, cored and thinly sliced

1 (4-ounce) package crumbled blue cheese

¼ cup chopped walnuts, toasted

1. Combine first 4 ingredients in a jar. Cover tightly, and shake vigorously.

2. Combine spinach and dressing in a large bowl, tossing gently. Divide spinach mixture evenly among 6 salad plates. Arrange endive leaves and apple slices beside spinach mixture.

3. To serve, sprinkle evenly with blue cheese and walnuts. **YIELD:** 6 servings (serving size: 1 cup spinach, about 1 cup endive, about 2 apple slices, 2½ tablespoons cheese, and 2 teaspoons walnuts).

CALORIES 135; FAT 8.9g (sat 3.9g, mono 1.9g, poly 2.6g); PROTEIN 6.8g; CARB 9.2g; FIBER 3.6g; CHOL 14mg; IRON 2mg; SODIUM 364mg; CALC 162mg

SENSATIONAL SALADS & SIDES

CHOICE INGREDIENT: *Blue cheese*

Semisoft cheeses, such as blue cheese, are also good eating cheeses. They make suitable accents for bread, salad, and salad dressings. The distinctive flavor of blue cheese drives people to either love it or hate it. Whether its source is goat's, cow's, or sheep's milk, a little blue packs a potent punch.

Colorful Coleslaw

1 (8.5-ounce) package preshredded coleslaw mix (6 cups)
1 cup frozen whole-kernel corn, thawed
¾ cup chopped red onion
¾ cup chopped red bell pepper
⅓ cup white vinegar
2 tablespoons "measures-like-sugar" calorie-free sweetener
1 teaspoon celery seeds
½ teaspoon salt
½ teaspoon chicken-flavored bouillon granules
¼ teaspoon mustard seeds
1 tablespoon water
2 teaspoons vegetable oil
Dash of hot sauce

1. Remove dressing packet from coleslaw mix; reserve for another use. Combine coleslaw mix and next 3 ingredients in a large bowl; toss well.

2. Combine vinegar and remaining 8 ingredients in a small saucepan. Bring to a boil, stirring constantly until sweetener dissolves. Pour over coleslaw mixture; toss well. Cover and chill at least 2 hours. Toss before serving. Serve with a slotted spoon.

YIELD: 5 servings (serving size: 1 cup).

CALORIES 131; FAT 2.4g (sat 0.4g, mono 0.6g, poly 1.4g); PROTEIN 2.2g; CARB 26.9g; FIBER 2.9g; CHOL 0mg; IRON 1mg; SODIUM 296mg; CALC 43mg

RECIPE BENEFITS: low-fat

Sweet Substitutions

There are several sugar substitutes on the market, and the best one to use is really a personal preference. However, we've found that some types of sweeteners work better in cooking than others.

HERE'S A LIST OF THE SWEETENERS WE USE AND WHAT THEY'RE CALLED:
• Splenda: "measures-like-sugar" calorie-free sweetener
• Equal: calorie-free sweetener with aspartame
• Equal Spoonful: "measures-like-sugar" calorie-free sweetener with aspartame
• Brown Sugar Twin: "measures-like-sugar" brown sugar calorie-free sweetener

Aspartame Safety

The Food and Drug Administration (FDA) approved the use of aspartame (sold under the trade names Equal and Nutrasweet) in all foods and beverages in 1996.

Although the sweetener has come under a lot of scrutiny due to reports that it caused symptoms such as headaches, dizziness, nausea, memory loss, and seizures and was responsible for the increased incidence of brain tumors, there is no scientific research to support these complaints. None of the leading health organizations in the United States has found a casual relationship between aspartame and the adverse effects listed above.

USING SUGAR SUBSTITUTES ON A DIABETIC EATING PLAN
When you love sweets and are trying to cut back on carbohydrate to help control your blood sugars, calorie-free sweeteners and sugar substitutes can help you enjoy sweet treats without adding carbohydrates that could increase your blood sugar.

In our diabetes-friendly recipes, you'll see that we use small amounts of a variety of sweeteners: calorie-free sweeteners, honey, fruit juices, and even real sugar.

BOTH THE AMERICAN DIETETIC ASSOCIATION AND THE AMERICAN
DIABETES ASSOCIATION CONSIDER FDA-APPROVED SUGAR SUBSTITUTES
A SAFE PART OF A CALORIE- OR CARBOHYDRATE-CONTROLLED DIET.

MAKE AHEAD

Broccoli Salad

Sweet and savory, creamy and crunchy—this all-purpose salad is one of our favorites.

8 cups broccoli florets, chopped	2 tablespoons tarragon vinegar
1 cup seedless grapes, halved	2 tablespoons slivered almonds, toasted
½ cup raisins	
3 green onions, thinly sliced	4 turkey-bacon slices, cooked and crumbled
⅔ cup light mayonnaise	

1. Combine first 4 ingredients in a large bowl. Combine mayonnaise and vinegar; stir into broccoli mixture. Cover and chill.
2. Stir in almonds and bacon just before serving. YIELD: 9 servings (serving size: ¾ cup).

CALORIES 91; FAT 2.7g (sat 0.2g, mono 0.7g, poly 1g); PROTEIN 3.2g; CARB 16.7g; FIBER 2.8g; CHOL 2mg; IRON 1mg; SODIUM 209mg; CALC 44mg

❋ RECIPE BENEFITS; low-carb

Marinated Tomato Slices

4 large red or yellow tomatoes, each cut into 4 slices	¼ teaspoon freshly ground black pepper
¼ cup lemon juice	1 garlic clove, minced
2 tablespoons minced red onion	Green leaf lettuce leaves (optional)
2 tablespoons red wine vinegar	
1 tablespoon chopped fresh basil or 1 teaspoon dried basil	

1. Arrange tomato slices in a large shallow dish. Combine lemon juice and next 5 ingredients; pour over tomato slices, turning to coat. Cover and marinate in refrigerator at least 2 hours.

2. Arrange tomato slices evenly on 8 lettuce-lined salad plates, if desired. Spoon marinade evenly over tomato slices. **YIELD:** 8 servings (serving size: 2 tomato slices and 1 tablespoon marinade).

CALORIES 21; FAT 0.2g (sat 0g, mono 0g, poly 0.1g); PROTEIN 1g; CARB 4.7g; FIBER 1.2g; CHOL 0mg; IRON 0.3mg; SODIUM 5mg; CALC 12mg

RECIPE BENEFITS: low-fat; low-sodium; low-carb

Count Carbs

CARBOHYDRATE is your body's preferred source of fuel. The brain depends exclusively on carbohydrate for its energy when that fuel is available. If there is no carbohydrate available (either from the foods that are eaten or in storage in the liver or muscles), the body will convert protein and/or fat to glucose (the form of carbohydrate the body uses for energy).

But if you eat more carbohydrate than your body needs for fuel, a small amount of it is stored in the liver or the muscles to be used later for energy. The rest of it gets changed and is stored in the body as fat.

Understanding Carbohydrate

IDEAL CARBOHYDRATE LEVEL

There's no specific recommended amount of carbohydrate. The amount of carbohydrate you need depends on many factors, including the following:

- current weight and height
- physical activity level
- gender
- health status
- diabetes medications

PREFERRED CARBOHYDRATE

Most diabetic eating plans don't completely restrict carbohydrate—they allow a specific amount of the right kinds of carbohydrate. The ideal carbohydrates in terms of weight loss and disease prevention have the following characteristics:

- high in fiber
- absorbed slowly
- do not cause rapid increase in blood glucose

The carbohydrates in fruits and vegetables are good for you because when you eat them, you get a whole package of disease-fighting vitamins and minerals. Fruits and vegetables, as well as whole grains and cereals, also contain carbohydrate in the form of fiber. Because fiber isn't digested by the body, these foods are absorbed slowly and don't cause a rapid rise in blood glucose. When the blood glucose rises slowly, the carbohydrate isn't stored as fat as easily.

Carbohydrates can be classified two ways: simple and complex. Simple carbohydrates are sugars such as glucose, sucrose, lactose, and fructose that are found in fruit and refined sugar.

Complex carbohydrates (or starches) are chains of simple sugars bonded together and are found in starches such as beans, vegetables, and whole grains. After they're digested by the body, complex carbohydrates (starches) are broken down into simple sugars. Complex carbohydrates are considered healthier because they contain fiber and are digested slower, providing a steady energy source.

See below for a general list of food groups that can impact blood glucose and those that usually don't. Some of the foods in the second group can increase blood sugar if they're eaten in large quantities.

FOOD GROUPS THAT CAN INCREASE BLOOD SUGAR

- Breads, cereals, pasta, rice
- Starchy vegetables
- Beans, peas, lentils
- Fruit
- Juice
- Regular soda, carbonated beverages
- Candy
- Chocolate
- Milk, yogurt

FOOD GROUPS THAT USUALLY DON'T INCREASE BLOOD SUGAR

- Meat
- Fats, oils, salad dressing*, butter, margarine
- Seeds, nuts, peanut butter*
- Cream cheese, sour cream
- Sugar-free hard candy and gum*
- Sugar substitutes
- Coffee, tea, sugar-free soft drinks
- Herbs and spices

*Check the label for carbohydrate content, because some products do contain a significant amount of carbohydrate.

Confetti Rice Salad

1 (10½-ounce) can low-sodium chicken broth
1 cup water
1 cup long-grain rice, uncooked
½ cup chopped carrot
¼ cup lemon juice
1 tablespoon olive oil
¾ cup chopped seeded plum tomato (about 2 medium)

¾ cup chopped cooked reduced-fat, low-salt ham
⅓ cup grated fresh Parmesan cheese
⅓ cup sliced green onions
⅓ cup chopped fresh parsley

1. Combine broth and water in a large saucepan; bring to a boil. Add rice and carrot; stir well. Reduce heat to low; cover and simmer 20 minutes or until liquid is absorbed and rice is tender.
2. Add lemon juice and oil to rice mixture; stir well. Add tomato and remaining ingredients; toss well. Transfer to a serving bowl. Cover and chill at least 2 hours. Stir just before serving. **YIELD:** 5 servings (serving size: 1 cup).

CALORIES 234; FAT 5.8g (sat 1.6g, mono 2.1g, poly 0.6g); PROTEIN 11g; CARB 34.6g; FIBER 1.8g; CHOL 14mg; IRON 3mg; SODIUM 470mg; CALC 144mg

Go with A Quick Grain

Cooking regular long-grain rice can take more than 20 minutes. To speed things up, try a quick-cooking rice. Here are the three most commonly available types:

• Boil-in-bag rice: The results from the brands we tested were comparable, regardless of whether the rice was cooked in the microwave or on the stovetop. The microwave method is faster, because you don't have to wait for water to boil on the stove.

• Instant rice: This rice takes half as much time to prepare as boil-in-bag rice; however, our instant rice tended to be mushy.

• Precooked rice in a pouch: Since the rice is already cooked, all you need to do is open the pouch and microwave for 60 to 90 seconds. Precooked rice contains oil to coat and separate the grains. Some of our staff liked the taste of the oil, while others thought it had an off flavor. Because some precooked rice products can contain as much as 500 milligrams of sodium per cup, be sure to check the labels.

KITCHEN TIP: Save leftover cooked rice. You can store it in a zip-top bag for up to three days. To reheat, simply put the rice in a wire-mesh colander and run under hot water for a few minutes to moisten and reheat. Drain and serve.

Hoppin' John Salad

2½ cups low-sodium chicken broth, divided
1 cup converted rice, uncooked
¼ cup apple cider vinegar
1½ teaspoons salt-free Cajun seasoning
2 teaspoons olive oil
½ teaspoon dried thyme
½ teaspoon minced garlic
¼ teaspoon hot sauce
1 (15.8-ounce) can black-eyed peas, drained
½ cup finely chopped celery
½ cup thinly sliced green onions
3 (1-ounce) slices lean ham, cut into thin strips
Fresh thyme (optional)

1. Place 2¼ cups broth in a medium saucepan; bring to a boil. Add rice, stirring well. Cover, reduce heat, and simmer 20 minutes. Remove from heat; let stand, covered, 5 minutes.

2. Combine remaining ¼ cup broth, vinegar, and next 5 ingredients in a small bowl.

3. Combine rice, peas, and next 3 ingredients in a large bowl. Add vinegar mixture, stirring gently to combine. Cover and chill at least 30 minutes. Garnish with fresh thyme, if desired. YIELD: 6 servings (serving size: 1 cup).

CALORIES 195; FAT 2.4g (sat 0.3g, mono 1.1g, poly 0.2g); PROTEIN 8.6g; CARB 34.4g; FIBER 2g; CHOL 8mg; IRON 1mg; SODIUM 558mg; CALC 27mg

Apple Cider Applesauce

8 cups sliced peeled cooking apple
(about 2½ pounds)
½ cup apple cider or apple juice
¼ cup "measures-like-sugar"
calorie-free sweetener

⅛ teaspoon ground nutmeg
¼ teaspoon ground cinnamon

1. Combine apple and apple cider in a large saucepan. Bring to a boil, stirring frequently; cover, reduce heat, and simmer 20 minutes or until apple is tender, stirring occasionally.

2. Add sweetener and nutmeg to apple mixture; stir. Cook until sweetener dissolves, stirring constantly. Mash apple mixture slightly with a potato masher until mixture is chunky. Cover and chill thoroughly. Sprinkle evenly with cinnamon before serving.

YIELD: 6 servings (serving size: ½ cup).

CALORIES 83; FAT 0.2g (sat 0g, mono 0g, poly 0.1g); PROTEIN 0.5g; CARB 21.7g; FIBER 2g; CHOL 0mg; IRON 0mg; SODIUM 0mg; CALC 9mg

RECIPE BENEFITS: low-fat; low-sodium

> **QUICK TIP:** Using a potato masher gets the best chunky texture for this applesauce. If you don't have a potato masher, use a fork.

Asparagus with Garlic Cream

Drizzle crisp-tender asparagus spears with a garlicky cream sauce and top with a sprinkling of fragrant snipped chives.

1 (8-ounce) carton reduced-fat sour cream
3 tablespoons fat-free milk
1 tablespoon white wine vinegar
⅛ teaspoon salt
⅛ teaspoon freshly ground black pepper
2 garlic cloves, minced
2 pounds fresh asparagus
2 teaspoons chopped fresh chives

1. Combine first 6 ingredients, stirring well. Cover and chill at least 2 hours.

2. Snap off tough ends of asparagus; remove scales from stalks with a vegetable peeler, if desired.

3. Place asparagus in a small amount of boiling water. Cover, reduce heat, and cook 4 minutes or until crisp-tender; drain. Plunge into ice water to stop the cooking process; drain. Cover and chill.

4. To serve, place asparagus on a serving platter. Top with sauce, and sprinkle with chives. **YIELD:** 8 servings (serving size: about 3 ounces asparagus and 2 tablespoons sauce).

CALORIES 64; FAT 3.5g (sat 2.2g, mono 0g, poly 0g); PROTEIN 3.1g; CARB 5.2g; FIBER 1.5g; CHOL 14mg; IRON 2mg; SODIUM 58mg; CALC 71mg

RECIPE BENEFITS: low-sodium; low-carb

Broccoli-Cheese Casserole

The seasoned stuffing mix makes a crunchy topping for the creamy broccoli mixture.

2 (10-ounce) packages frozen broccoli spears
Butter-flavored cooking spray
1 cup (4 ounces) shredded reduced-fat sharp Cheddar cheese
½ cup egg substitute
½ cup fat-free mayonnaise
½ cup finely chopped onion
1 (10 ¾-ounce) can condensed reduced-fat, reduced-sodium cream of mushroom soup, undiluted
1 (6-ounce) box reduced-sodium chicken-flavored stuffing mix

1. Preheat oven to 350°.

2. Cook broccoli according to package directions; drain. Arrange broccoli in an 11- x 7-inch baking dish coated with cooking spray. Sprinkle with cheese. Combine egg substitute and next 3 ingredients; spread over cheese.

3. Combine ¾ cup stuffing mix and 2½ teaspoons of the mix's seasoning packet, tossing well. Sprinkle over casserole; coat with cooking spray. (Reserve remaining stuffing mix and seasoning packet for another use.)

4. Bake at 350° for 30 minutes or until thoroughly heated. Serve warm. **YIELD:** 8 servings (serving size: about 1 cup).

CALORIES 192; FAT 6.4g (sat 2.8g, mono 0.7g, poly 1.0g); PROTEIN 10.8g; CARB 23.8g; FIBER 3.4g; CHOL 13mg; IRON 2mg; SODIUM 685mg; CALC 162mg

Green Beans with Bacon

2½ pounds green beans, trimmed
3 bacon slices
½ cup chopped shallots
1 teaspoon freshly squeezed
lemon juice

¼ teaspoon salt
¼ teaspoon freshly ground black
pepper

1. Cook green beans in boiling water 5 minutes or until crisp-tender. Drain and plunge beans into ice water; drain.
2. Cook bacon in a Dutch oven over medium heat until crisp. Remove bacon from pan; crumble. Add shallots to drippings in pan; sauté 4 minutes or until tender. Add beans, juice, salt, and pepper to pan; toss to combine. Cook 5 minutes or until thoroughly heated, stirring often. Remove from heat. Sprinkle bacon over bean mixture; toss. **YIELD:** 12 servings (serving size: about ⅔ cup).

CALORIES 46; FAT 1.1g (sat 0.4g, mono 0.5g, poly 0.2g); PROTEIN 2.5g; CARB 8g; FIBER 3.3g; CHOL 2mg; IRON 1.1mg; SODIUM 93mg; CALC 38mg

RECIPE BENEFITS: low-fat; low-sodium; low-carb

Orange-Glazed Carrots

1 pound carrots, scraped and cut into ¼-inch-thick slices
¾ cup fat-free, less-sodium chicken broth
2 tablespoons frozen orange juice concentrate

2 teaspoons "measures-like-sugar" calorie-free sweetener
¼ teaspoon ground ginger

1. Combine carrot and broth in a medium saucepan; bring to a boil. Cover, reduce heat, and simmer 10 minutes.

2. Add orange juice concentrate, sweetener, and ginger to carrot mixture, stirring well. Cook, uncovered, over medium heat 8 minutes or until carrot is tender and liquid is reduced, stirring occasionally.

3. Serve immediately. **YIELD:** 4 servings (serving size: ½ cup).

CALORIES 68; FAT 0.2g (sat 0g, mono 0g, poly 0.1g); PROTEIN 1.5g; CARB 16.0g; FIBER 3.3g; CHOL 0mg; IRON 1mg; SODIUM 197mg; CALC 41mg

RECIPE BENEFITS: low-fat; low-sodium

> **QUICK TIP:** If your carrots have gone limp, soak them in ice water for 20 to 30 minutes until they are crisp again.

Corn Pudding

¼ cup "measures-like-sugar" calorie-free sweetener
¼ cup all-purpose flour
2 teaspoons baking powder
½ teaspoon salt
2 cups fat-free evaporated milk
1½ cups egg substitute
2 tablespoons margarine, melted
6 cups fresh corn kernels (about 12 ears)
Cooking spray

1. Preheat oven to 350°.

2. Combine first 4 ingredients; set aside.

3. Combine milk, egg substitute, and margarine in a large bowl. Gradually add flour mixture, stirring until smooth. Stir in corn. Pour mixture into a 13- x 9-inch baking dish coated with cooking spray.

4. Bake, uncovered, at 350° for 40 to 45 minutes or until deep golden and set. Let stand 5 minutes before serving. **YIELD:** 16 servings (serving size: ½ cup).

CALORIES 112; FAT 2.8g (sat 0.5g, mono 1.1g, poly 1.1g); PROTEIN 6.9g; CARB 16.4g; FIBER 1.6g; CHOL 0mg; IRON 1mg; SODIUM 235mg; CALC 128mg

RECIPE BENEFITS: low-fat

INGREDIENT TIP: If fresh corn is out of season, you can use thawed and drained frozen whole-kernel corn.

Roasted New Potatoes

Enjoy these crispy Parmesan cheese-coated potatoes instead of high-fat French fries.

24 small round red potatoes (about 2⅓ pounds)
Olive oil-flavored cooking spray
¼ cup Italian-seasoned breadcrumbs
¼ cup grated fresh Parmesan cheese
¾ teaspoon paprika

1. Place potatoes in a Dutch oven; add water to cover. Bring to a boil; reduce heat, and cook, uncovered, 15 minutes or until tender; drain and cool slightly.

2. Preheat oven to 450°.

3. Quarter potatoes; coat with cooking spray. Combine breadcrumbs, cheese, and paprika; sprinkle over potatoes, tossing to coat well. Arrange in a single layer on a baking sheet coated with cooking spray. Bake at 450° for 20 to 25 minutes or until coating is crispy. **YIELD:** 8 servings (serving size: 12 potato quarters).

CALORIES 123; FAT 1.5g (sat 0.6g, mono 0g, poly 0.1g); PROTEIN 4.5g; CARB 23.6g; FIBER 2.4g; CHOL 3mg; IRON 1mg; SODIUM 127mg; CALC 69mg

RECIPE BENEFITS: low-fat; low-sodium

Grilled Summer Squash with Rosemary

Bright yellow squash is packed with such disease-fighting nutrients as vitamins A and C. And because you eat the skin and the seeds, it's a good source of fiber.

1 pound yellow squash	1 tablespoon olive oil
2 tablespoons balsamic vinegar	¼ teaspoon salt
1 tablespoon chopped fresh rosemary	Olive oil-flavored cooking spray

1. Prepare grill.

2. Cut squash in half lengthwise. Combine vinegar and next 3 ingredients in a large bowl. Add squash, and toss to coat.

3. Place squash on grill rack coated with cooking spray; cover and grill 8 to 10 minutes or until tender, turning and basting with rosemary mixture every 2 minutes. **YIELD:** 4 servings.

CALORIES 58; FAT 4g (sat 0.6g, mono 2.5g, poly 0.6g); PROTEIN 1.4g; CARB 5.4g; FIBER 1.3g; CHOL 0mg; IRON 1mg; SODIUM 150mg; CALC 25mg

RECIPE BENEFITS: low-carb

Sweet potatoes are rich in beta-carotene, vitamin C, and vitamin E—nutrients that can help prevent heart disease and certain cancers.

Orange Sweet Potatoes

3 medium sweet potatoes	1 tablespoon light butter, melted
⅔ cup orange juice	¼ teaspoon ground cinnamon

1. Preheat oven to 400°.

2. Peel sweet potatoes, and cut lengthwise into ¼-inch-thick slices. Arrange potato slices in a single layer in a 13- x 9-inch baking dish. Combine orange juice, margarine, and cinnamon in a small bowl, stirring well. Pour over sweet potato slices. Bake, uncovered, at 400° for 30 minutes or until tender, turning once.

YIELD: 8 servings (serving size: about 4 slices).

CALORIES 60; FAT 0.1g (sat 0.6g, mono 0.3g, poly 0.1g); PROTEIN 1g; CARB 12g; FIBER 1.5g; CHOL 2mg; IRON 0.4mg; SODIUM 34mg; CALC 19mg

RECIPE BENEFITS: low-fat; low-sodium

Brown Rice Pilaf

2 cups fat-free, less-sodium chicken broth	¼ teaspoon ground red pepper
1 cup uncooked brown rice	1 garlic clove, minced
½ cup shredded carrot	¼ cup thinly sliced green onions
½ cup finely chopped celery	3 tablespoons slivered almonds, toasted
½ teaspoon salt	

1. Bring broth to a boil in a heavy saucepan; stir in rice and next 5 ingredients. Cover, reduce heat, and simmer 50 to 55 minutes or until rice is tender and liquid is absorbed. Stir in green onions and almonds. **YIELD:** 8 servings (serving size: ½ cup).

CALORIES 110; FAT 2g (sat 0.3g, mono 1.1g, poly 0.6g); PROTEIN 3.5g; CARB 19.9g; FIBER 2.1g; CHOL 0mg; IRON 1mg; SODIUM 303mg; CALC 22mg

RECIPE BENEFITS: low-fat

Main Dish Must-Haves

Cedar Plank-Grilled Salmon with Avocado-Orange Salsa

1 (15 x 6½ x ⅜-inch) cedar grilling plank
¼ cup maple syrup
2 tablespoons Cointreau (orange-flavored liqueur)
1 teaspoon grated orange rind
½ teaspoon salt, divided
¼ teaspoon freshly ground black pepper, divided
6 (6-ounce) salmon fillets (about 1 inch thick)
1 cup orange sections (about 2 oranges)
¾ cup diced peeled avocado (about 1)
¼ cup fresh orange juice (about 1 orange)
2 tablespoons finely chopped red onion
2 tablespoons finely chopped red bell pepper
1 tablespoon finely chopped fresh chives
1 tablespoon fresh lime juice

1. Immerse and soak the plank in water 1 hour; drain.
2. Prepare grill.
3. Combine syrup, Cointreau, and rind in a small saucepan; bring to a boil. Cook until reduced to ¼ cup (about 3 minutes). Cool 5 minutes. Sprinkle ¼ teaspoon salt and ⅛ teaspoon black pepper over fish; brush fish with syrup mixture.
4. Place plank on grill rack, and grill for 3 minutes or until lightly charred. Carefully turn plank over, and place fish on charred side of plank. Cover and grill for 12 minutes or until fish flakes easily when tested with a fork or until desired degree of doneness.
5. Combine remaining ¼ teaspoon salt, remaining ⅛ teaspoon black pepper, orange sections, avocado, orange juice, onion, bell pepper, chives, and lime juice in a medium bowl; serve with fish.
YIELD: 6 servings (serving size: 1 salmon fillet and ¼ cup salsa).

CALORIES 425; FAT 21.5g (sat 4.2g, mono 8.4g, poly 7.1g); PROTEIN 34.8g; CARB 19.8g; FIBER 2.2g; CHOL 100mg; IRON 1.1mg; SODIUM 298mg; CALC 55mg

Stocking Up

Use this handy list to keep your kitchen stocked with the basic ingredients you need for quick low-fat, low-sugar cooking.

CHECK THE PANTRY FOR THESE STAPLES:

- ☐ Baking powder
- ☐ Baking soda
- ☐ Bouillon granules: chicken, beef, and vegetable
- ☐ Broth, canned: reduced-sodium chicken, beef, vegetable
- ☐ Cornstarch
- ☐ Flour: all-purpose, self-rising, whole wheat
- ☐ Milk: nonfat dry milk powder, fat-free evaporated
- ☐ Oats: quick cooking
- ☐ Oils: olive, sesame, and vegetable
- ☐ Sugar substitutes and sugar
- ☐ Unflavored gelatin and sugar-free gelatin mixes

KEEP THESE FRUITS AND VEGETABLES ON HAND:

- ☐ Canned beans
- ☐ Canned tomato products: paste, sauce, whole, diced, and seasoned tomatoes
- ☐ Canned vegetables
- ☐ Canned fruits packed in juice
- ☐ Dried fruits

YOU CAN ALWAYS MAKE A MEAL WHEN YOU HAVE THESE GRAINS AND PASTAS:

- ☐ Bulgur
- ☐ Couscous
- ☐ Dry pastas
- ☐ Rice and rice blends
- ☐ Dry cereals without added sugar

ADD FLAVOR WITH THESE CONDIMENTS AND SEASONINGS:

- ☐ Bottled minced garlic
- ☐ Dried herbs and spices
- ☐ Mayonnaise, low-fat
- ☐ Mustards
- ☐ Salad dressings and vinaigrettes: fat-free and reduced-fat
- ☐ Seasoning sauces: hot sauce, ketchup, low-sodium soy sauce, Worcestershire sauce
- ☐ Vinegars

FILL THE FRIDGE WITH THESE ITEMS:

- ☐ Cheeses, reduced-fat
- ☐ Eggs and egg substitute
- ☐ Milk: fat-free milk and low-fat buttermilk
- ☐ Margarine, reduced-calorie margarine, and light butter
- ☐ Rolls and pizza dough
- ☐ Sour cream, low-fat
- ☐ Yogurt, low-fat

STOCK UP AND STORE THESE FOODS IN THE FREEZER:

- ☐ Cooked chicken: diced or strips
- ☐ Ground round, pork chops, other meats
- ☐ Frozen fruits
- ☐ Frozen vegetables
- ☐ Juice concentrates

MAIN DISH MUST-HAVES

Dilled Shrimp with Angel Hair Pasta

6 ounces uncooked angel hair pasta	1 pound peeled and deveined large shrimp
2 tablespoons light stick butter	½ cup fat-free half-and-half or fat-free evaporated milk
¾ cup sliced green onions (about 3 large)	¼ cup tub-style light cream cheese
3 tablespoons fresh lemon juice (1 large lemon)	2 tablespoons chopped fresh dill or 1½ teaspoons dried dill
2 large garlic cloves, minced	

1. Cook pasta according to package directions; omit salt and fat.

2. Melt butter in a large nonstick skillet over medium-high heat. Add green onions, lemon juice, and garlic; sauté 2 minutes. Add shrimp, and cook 5 minutes or until shrimp are done. Remove shrimp from skillet.

3. Add half-and-half, cream cheese, and dill to pan, stirring until smooth. Cook 1 to 2 minutes or until mixture is bubbly. Return shrimp to pan, and cook until thoroughly heated. Drain pasta; stir in shrimp mixture, and serve immediately. **YIELD:** 4 servings (serving size: about 1¼ cups).

CALORIES 329; FAT 7.5g (sat 4g, mono 1.3g, poly 2g); PROTEIN 25.7g; CARB 38.3g; FIBER 2g; CHOL 183mg; IRON 4.2mg; SODIUM 351mg; CALC 100mg

CHOICE INGREDIENT: *Dill*

Since ancient Roman times, dill has been a symbol of vitality. In the Middle Ages, it was thought to provide protection against witches and was used as an ingredient in many magic potions. In the kitchen, its feathery leaves lend a fresh, sharp flavor to all kinds of foods. If you don't have fresh dill, this is an herb that maintains good flavor when it's dried. Substitute 3 teaspoons dried dill for 3 tablespoons fresh.

Broiled Red Snapper with Sicilian Tomato Pesto

PESTO:
- 2 cups basil leaves
- 2 tablespoons pine nuts, toasted
- 2 tablespoons extra-virgin olive oil
- 2 garlic cloves, minced
- ¼ cup (1 ounce) grated Parmigiano-Reggiano cheese
- ⅛ teaspoon crushed red pepper
- 1½ cups chopped plum tomato (about 3 medium)
- ½ teaspoon salt
- ½ teaspoon freshly ground black pepper

FISH:
- 6 (6-ounce) red snapper or other firm whitefish fillets
- ¼ teaspoon salt
- Cooking spray

REMAINING INGREDIENT:
- 3 cups hot cooked orzo

1. To prepare pesto, combine first 4 ingredients in a food processor; process until smooth. Add cheese and red pepper; process until blended. Transfer mixture to a bowl. Add tomato, ½ teaspoon salt, and black pepper, stirring gently to combine.

2. Preheat broiler.

3. To prepare fish, sprinkle fish with ¼ teaspoon salt. Arrange fish on a broiler pan coated with cooking spray, and broil 8 minutes or until fish flakes easily when tested with a fork. Place ½ cup orzo on each of 6 plates, and top each serving with 1 fillet and ¼ cup pesto. **YIELD:** 6 servings (serving size: ½ cup orzo, 1 fillet and ¼ cup pesto).

CALORIES 437; FAT 10.8g (sat 2.4g, mono 4.8g, poly 2g); PROTEIN 44.9g; CARB 38.9g; FIBER 3.1g; CHOL 67mg; IRON 2.9mg; SODIUM 497mg; CALC 156mg

MAKE-AHEAD TIP: You can make the pesto ahead and keep it chilled. Stir in the tomatoes just before serving.

Seared Mediterranean Tuna Steaks

Coriander has a lemon-sage flavor that complements the tuna and the fresh tomato sauce. Serve with a side of refrigerated potato wedges, roasted according to package instructions. See page 59 for more info on Yellowfin tuna steaks.

4 (6-ounce) Yellowfin tuna steaks (about ¾ inch thick)
½ teaspoon salt, divided
½ teaspoon ground coriander
⅛ teaspoon black pepper
Cooking spray
1½ cups chopped seeded tomato
¼ cup chopped green onions

3 tablespoons chopped fresh parsley
1 tablespoon capers, drained
1 tablespoon extra-virgin olive oil
1 tablespoon lemon juice
½ teaspoon bottled minced garlic
12 chopped pitted kalamata olives

1. Heat a large nonstick skillet over medium-high heat. Sprinkle fish with ¼ teaspoon salt, coriander, and pepper. Coat pan with cooking spray. Add fish to pan; cook 4 minutes on each side or until desired degree of doneness.

2. While fish cooks, combine remaining ¼ teaspoon salt, tomato, and remaining ingredients. Serve tomato mixture over fish. YIELD: 4 servings (serving size: 1 tuna steak and ⅔ cup tomato mixture).

CALORIES 268; FAT 8.4g (sat 1.3g, mono 5.3g, poly 1.2g); PROTEIN 40.9g; CARB 5.8g; FIBER 1.4g; CHOL 77mg; IRON 2mg; SODIUM 610mg; CALC 48mg

RECIPE BENEFIT: low-carb

How Much Is a Serving?

FOR MANY PEOPLE, CONTROLLING PORTIONS IS THE BIGGEST CHALLENGE IN CONTROLLING DIABETES. Whether you are counting carbohydrate or watching portion sizes in order to lose weight, the guide below will help you see in your mind's eye the appropriate serving size for each of a variety of foods.

MAIN DISH MUST-HAVES

1 ounce cooked meat, poultry, or fish	=	Matchbook
3 ounces cooked meat, poultry, or fish	=	Deck of playing cards, cassette tape, or the palm of a woman's hand
1 slice cheese	=	3.5-inch computer disk
1 ounce cheese	=	4 dice or a tube of lipstick
2 tablespoons peanut butter	=	Golf ball
1 standard bagel	=	Hockey puck or 6-ounce can of tuna
1 cup potatoes, rice, or pasta	=	Size of a fist or a tennis ball
1 medium potato	=	Computer mouse or 1 small bar of soap
½ cup cooked vegetables	=	6 asparagus spears, 7 to 8 baby carrots or carrot sticks, 1 ear of corn, or 3 spears broccoli
½ cup chopped fresh vegetables	=	3 regular ice cubes
1 cup chopped fresh leafy greens	=	4 lettuce leaves
1 medium orange or apple, or 1 cup fruit or yogurt	=	Baseball

Source: National Center for Nutrition and Dietetics of The American Dietetic Association and its Foundation, ADAF

Veggie-Bean Tostadas

Cooking spray
1½ cups presliced mushrooms
1½ cups packaged fresh broccoli florets
1 cup packaged shredded carrot
½ cup picante sauce
2 tablespoons water
1 (16-ounce) can fat-free refried beans

4 (6-inch) corn tortillas
1 cup (4 ounces) preshredded reduced-fat Mexican blend or Cheddar cheese
1½ tablespoons fat-free sour cream (optional)
¼ cup chopped fresh cilantro (optional)
½ cup picante sauce (optional)

1. Coat a large nonstick skillet with cooking spray; place over medium-high heat until hot. Add mushrooms and next 4 ingredients; cover and simmer 7 minutes or until vegetables are crisp-tender.

2. Heat beans according to directions on label.

3. Preheat broiler. Place tortillas on baking sheet; broil 1 minute on each side or until crisp and golden. Place tortillas on individual serving plates. Top with beans, vegetables, cheese, and, if desired, sour cream, cilantro, and picante sauce. **YIELD:** 4 servings.

CALORIES 242; FAT 5.3g (sat 3g, mono 0.8g, poly 1.1g); PROTEIN 17.8g; CARB 34.1g; FIBER 8g; CHOL 10mg; IRON 0.6mg; SODIUM 846mg; CALC 228mg

RECIPE BENEFIT: high-fiber

Tomato-Basil Pizza

For a quick meal, serve this pizza with a fruit salad or a piece of fresh fruit.

1 (10-ounce) Italian cheese-flavored pizza thin crust (such as Boboli)
⅓ cup pizza sauce
2 ripe tomatoes, thinly sliced

2 teaspoons dried basil or 2 tablespoons chopped fresh basil
¼ cup grated Parmesan cheese
1 cup (4 ounces) preshredded part-skim mozzarella cheese

1. Preheat oven to 450°.
2. Place crust on a baking sheet; spread with pizza sauce. Top crust with tomato slices; sprinkle with basil and Parmesan cheese.
3. Bake at 450° for 10 minutes. Sprinkle with mozzarella cheese; bake 2 to 3 minutes or until crust is golden and cheese melts.
4. Cut into 8 wedges. YIELD: 4 servings (serving size: 2 wedges).

CALORIES 345; FAT 11.9g (sat 6.4g, mono 3.4g, poly 1.6g); PROTEIN 17.9g; CARB 41.3g; FIBER 3g; CHOL 20mg; IRON 3mg; SODIUM 679mg; CALC 395mg

Artichoke Quiche

- 2 cups cooked long-grain rice (cooked without salt or fat)
- ¾ cup (3 ounces) shredded reduced-fat sharp Cheddar cheese, divided
- ¾ cup fat-free egg substitute, divided
- 1 teaspoon dried dillweed
- ½ teaspoon salt
- 1 small garlic clove, crushed
- Cooking spray
- 1 (14-ounce) can quartered artichoke hearts, drained
- ¾ cup fat-free milk
- ¼ cup sliced green onions
- 1 tablespoon Dijon mustard
- ¼ teaspoon ground white pepper
- Green onion strips (optional)

1. Combine rice, ¼ cup cheese, ¼ cup fat-free egg substitute, dillweed, salt, and garlic; press into a 9-inch pieplate coated with cooking spray. Bake at 350° for 5 minutes.

2. Arrange artichoke quarters on bottom of rice crust; sprinkle evenly with remaining ½ cup cheese. Combine remaining ½ cup egg substitute, milk, and next 3 ingredients; pour over cheese.

3. Bake at 350° for 50 minutes or until set. Let stand 5 minutes; cut into wedges. Garnish with green onion strips, if desired.

YIELD: 6 servings.

CALORIES 161; FAT 3.2g (sat 2g, mono 0.6g, poly 0.5g); PROTEIN 10.2g; CARB 21.1g; FIBER 0g; CHOL 10mg; IRON 1.9mg; SODIUM 555mg; CALC 154mg

Low-Fat Substitutions

Here are a few simple reduced-fat substitutions for high-fat ingredients.

INGREDIENT	SUBSTITUTION
FATS & OILS	
Butter	Light butter, reduced-calorie margarine (except for baking)
Margarine	Light butter, reduced-calorie margarine (except for baking)
Mayonnaise	Fat-free, light, or low-fat mayonnaise
Oil	Polyunsaturated or monounsaturated oil in a reduced amount (canola, olive)
Salad Dressing	Fat-free or reduced-fat salad dressing or vinaigrette
Shortening	Polyunsaturated or monounsaturated oil in a reduced amount
MEAT & POULTRY	
Bacon	Reduced-fat bacon; turkey bacon; lean ham; Canadian bacon
Ground Beef	Ground round, extra-lean ground beef, or ground turkey
Sausage	50%-less-fat pork sausage; turkey sausage
Luncheon Meat	Sliced turkey, chicken, lean roast beef, or lean ham
Tuna Packed in Oil	Tuna packed in water
Egg, whole	2 egg whites or ¼ cup egg substitute
DAIRY	
Sour Cream	Fat-free or reduced-fat sour cream; fat-free or low-fat plain yogurt
Cheese	Reduced-fat cheeses (or use less of the regular cheese)
Cottage Cheese	Fat-free or 1% low-fat cottage cheese
Ricotta Cheese	Part-skim or fat-free ricotta
Whole Milk	Fat-free or skim milk; 1% low-fat milk
Evaporated Milk	Fat-free evaporated milk
Half-and-Half	Fat-free half-and-half or fat-free evaporated milk
Whipped Cream	Fat-free or reduced-calorie frozen whipped topping
Ice Cream	Fat-free or low-fat ice cream or frozen yogurt; sherbet; sorbet
Soups, canned	Low-fat, reduced-sodium soups
OTHER	
Fudge Sauce	Fat-free chocolate syrup
Nuts	A reduced amount of nuts (one-third to one-half less)
Unsweetened Chocolate, 1 ounce	3 tablespoons unsweetened cocoa and 1 tablespoon butter

MAIN DISH MUST-HAVES

Baked Ravioli and Vegetables

10 cups water
1 (9-ounce) package refrigerated light cheese-filled ravioli
1 (16-ounce) package frozen broccoli, cauliflower, and carrots
1 (12-ounce) can fat-free evaporated milk, divided
2 tablespoons all-purpose flour
1 teaspoon dried Italian seasoning
½ teaspoon minced garlic
¼ teaspoon salt
¼ teaspoon ground pepper
¾ cup shredded fresh Parmesan cheese, divided
Cooking spray
2 tablespoons fine, dry breadcrumbs

1. Bring water to a boil in a Dutch oven. Add pasta and vegetables; cook 5 minutes. Drain.

2. Combine ½ cup milk and flour; stir well. Combine flour mixture, remaining milk, Italian seasoning, and next 3 ingredients in a saucepan. Cook over medium heat, stirring constantly, until thickened and bubbly. Stir in ½ cup Parmesan cheese.

3. Combine pasta mixture and cheese sauce; stir. Spoon into an 11 x 7-inch baking dish coated with cooking spray. Sprinkle with breadcrumbs. Bake at 350° for 15 minutes. Sprinkle remaining ¼ cup cheese over breadcrumbs; bake 5 minutes or until lightly browned. **YIELD:** 6 servings.

CALORIES 254; FAT 6.1g (sat 3.3g, mono 1.4g, poly 1.4g); PROTEIN 15.4g; CARB 34g; FIBER 3g; CHOL 29mg; IRON 1.2mg; SODIUM 602mg; CALC 360mg

Speedy Shepherd's Pie

½ (22-ounce) package frozen mashed potatoes (about 3 cups)
1⅓ cups fat-free milk
1 pound ground round
1 cup fresh or frozen chopped onion
1 cup frozen peas and carrots
½ teaspoon pepper
1 (12-ounce) jar fat-free beef gravy
½ cup (2 ounces) reduced-fat shredded Cheddar cheese

1. Combine potato and milk in a microwave-safe bowl. Microwave at HIGH, uncovered, 8 minutes, stirring once.

2. Cook beef and onion in a 10-inch ovenproof skillet over medium heat until beef is browned, stirring to crumble. Add peas and carrots, pepper, and gravy. Cook over medium heat 3 minutes or until thoroughly heated, stirring often. Remove from heat.

3. Spoon potato evenly over beef mixture, leaving a 1-inch border around edge of pan. Broil 3 minutes or until bubbly. Sprinkle with cheese; let stand 5 minutes. **YIELD:** 6 servings.

CALORIES 296; FAT 12g (sat 5.2g, mono 4.4g, poly 1.4g); PROTEIN 24g; CARB 24g; FIBER 3g; CHOL 59mg; IRON 2mg; SODIUM 559mg; CALC 150mg

All About Beef

Here are some of the most common questions consumers have about America's favorite red meat. Get the answers to help you add depth and versatility to your cooking.

WHAT ARE *COOKING LIGHT* MAGAZINE'S FAVORITE CUTS?

Two cuts show up repeatedly. Tenderloin is the most tender, luxurious cut you can buy, and it's very lean. Roasted whole, it's the ideal entrée for a celebratory dinner. Cut into filets and pan-seared, it's a superb supper for two. Cut into cubes, it makes outstanding kebabs on the grill.

Flank steak is one of those tough-but-superflavorful cuts, and it has a little more fat than tenderloin. Sear flank steak quickly and slice thinly, or braise slowly and shred. Its flat shape and coarse grain absorb flavors quickly, making it a good candidate for marinades.

GRADES OF BEEF: WHAT DO THEY MEAN, AND WHAT SHOULD YOU LOOK FOR?

USDA grading has nothing to do with food safety; it's a measure of taste. The two most important factors in grading are the age of the animal and the marbling in the meat. Beef can be given one of eight grades, but only the top three—Prime, Choice, and Select—are sold in supermarkets and butcher shops. Restaurants buy up most of the Prime meat, so supermarkets sell mostly Choice and Select. Look for Choice when tenderness and juiciness matter most, such as for oven roasts or thick steaks for grilling. For pot roast or stew meat, Select is fine.

WHAT SHOULD YOU LOOK FOR WHEN BUYING MEAT?

Beef should have a cherry red or—if it's vacuum-packed—a dark, purplish-red color; avoid meat with gray or brown blotches. The visible fat should be very white. Seek a moist surface and a fresh smell. Avoid packaged meat with a lot of liquid in the tray—that's usually a sign the meat has been frozen and thawed.

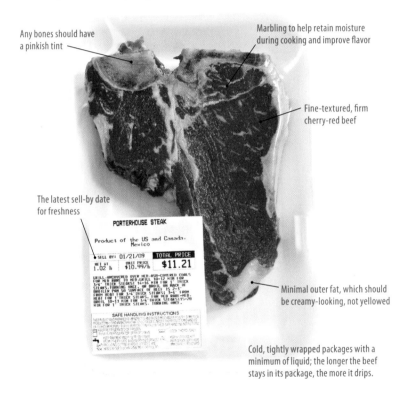

Any bones should have a pinkish tint

Marbling to help retain moisture during cooking and improve flavor

Fine-textured, firm cherry-red beef

The latest sell-by date for freshness

Minimal outer fat, which should be creamy-looking, not yellowed

Cold, tightly wrapped packages with a minimum of liquid; the longer the beef stays in its package, the more it drips.

HOW LONG CAN YOU KEEP BEEF IN THE REFRIGERATOR OR FREEZER?

Tightly wrapped and refrigerated, raw beef will last three to four days (ground beef, one to two days). At that point, it should be cooked or frozen. Cooked, it will keep in the refrigerator three to four days longer; frozen, it's best used within two months.

Beef Fajitas

Make your meal a fiesta: serve the fajitas with warm black beans
sprinkled with reduced-fat shredded Monterey Jack cheese.

1 (1-pound) lean flank steak
Cooking spray
½ cup bottled chili sauce
1 tablespoon no-salt-added Creole
  seasoning

3 cups onion strips
3 cups green, red, and yellow bell
  pepper strips
6 (8-inch) low-fat flour tortillas
Fresh cilantro sprigs (optional)

1. Cut steak diagonally across the grain into ¼-inch-thick slices.
Coat a large nonstick skillet with cooking spray, and place over
medium-high heat until hot. Add steak, chili sauce, and Creole
seasoning; cook 4 minutes or until meat is done. Remove from
pan. Add onion and bell pepper; sauté 7 minutes or until tender.
2. Wrap tortillas in wax paper; microwave at HIGH 30 seconds.
Spoon steak and vegetable mixture over warm tortillas; wrap or
fold tortillas around mixture. Garnish with cilantro sprigs, if
desired. **YIELD:** 6 servings.

CALORIES 297; FAT 5.8g (sat 1.6g, mono 1.5g, poly 1.2g); PROTEIN 21.4g; CARB 41g; FIBER 5g; CHOL 25mg;
IRON 3.3mg; SODIUM 682mg; CALC 135mg

Steak au Poivre

1 tablespoon cracked black pepper	½ cup fat-free, less-sodium beef
2 (4-ounce) beef tenderloin steaks	broth
(1 inch thick)	¼ teaspoon salt
Cooking spray	¼ teaspoon sugar
¼ cup brandy	3 tablespoons light sour cream

1. Press cracked black pepper evenly onto both sides of steaks.
2. Place a large nonstick skillet coated with cooking spray over medium-high heat until hot. Add steaks, and cook 5 minutes on each side or to desired degree of doneness. Transfer to a serving platter; set aside, and keep warm.
3. Add brandy to pan; let simmer 30 seconds or until liquid is reduced to a glaze. Add beef broth, salt, and sugar. Simmer, uncovered, 4 to 5 minutes or until liquid is reduced by half.
4. Remove pan from heat; stir in sour cream. Spoon warm sour cream mixture over steaks. **YIELD:** 2 servings (serving size: 1 steak and 2 tablespoons sauce).

CALORIES 258; FAT 9g (sat 3.9g, mono 3.08g, poly 0.53g); PROTEIN 19.5g; CARB 5.6g; FIBER 1g; CHOL 61mg; IRON 2.6mg; SODIUM 463mg; CALC 16mg

RECIPE BENEFIT: low-carb

Quick-and-Easy Salisbury Steaks

1 **pound ground round**
¼ **teaspoon garlic powder**
¼ **teaspoon salt**
¼ **teaspoon ground pepper**
Cooking spray
1 **(8-ounce) package presliced fresh mushrooms**
¼ **cup chopped onion**

1 **tablespoon finely chopped fresh thyme or 1 teaspoon dried thyme**
2 **tablespoons dry sherry or white wine**
1 **(12-ounce) jar fat-free beef gravy**
Fresh thyme sprigs (optional)

1. Combine first 4 ingredients in a medium bowl; mix well. Shape mixture into 4 (½-inch-thick) patties.

2. Coat a large nonstick skillet with cooking spray; place over medium heat until hot. Add patties, and cook 4 to 5 minutes on each side or until done. Remove patties from skillet, and set aside.

3. Increase heat to medium-high; add mushrooms, onion, and thyme; sauté 3 minutes or until vegetables are tender. Add sherry; cook 1 minute. Stir in gravy; return patties to skillet. Cook 2 minutes or until thoroughly heated. Garnish with thyme, if desired. **YIELD:** 4 servings.

CALORIES 251; FAT 11.6g (sat 4.6g, mono 4.9g, poly 0.5g); PROTEIN 27.5g; CARB 7.5g; FIBER 1g; CHOL 74mg; IRON 3mg; SODIUM 720mg; CALC 22mg

RECIPE BENEFIT: low-carb

SAFETY TIP: The U.S. Department of Agriculture (USDA) recommends that no matter what type of meat or poultry you're cooking in a slow cooker, turn the heat to high for the first hour. It creates steam and gets the food cooking quicker. The strategy is aimed at bringing cooking temperatures up to levels needed to prevent the growth of bacteria.

Slow-Cooked Beef Burgundy

¼ cup all-purpose flour
½ teaspoon salt
½ teaspoon ground pepper
2 pounds lean, boneless round steak, cut into 1½-inch pieces
1 teaspoon minced garlic
¾ cup dry red wine
¾ cup fat-free, less-sodium beef broth
1 tablespoon tomato paste
1 tablespoon chopped fresh thyme or 1 teaspoon dried thyme

8 ounces baby carrots (about 40 small)
1 large onion, cut into eighths
1 bay leaf
1 (8-ounce) package sliced fresh mushrooms
4 cups hot cooked yolk-free medium egg noodles (cooked without salt or fat)

1. Combine first 3 ingredients in a heavy-duty, zip-top plastic bag; add beef, and seal bag. Shake to coat. Place a large nonstick skillet over medium-high heat until hot. Add garlic and beef; cook 10 minutes or until browned on all sides, stirring often.

2. Transfer beef to a 4-quart electric slow cooker. Add wine and next 6 ingredients. Cover and cook on high setting 6 hours. Or cover and cook on high setting 1 hour; reduce to low setting, and cook 7 hours. Add mushrooms 1 hour before cooking is completed. Discard bay leaf. Stir. Spoon beef mixture evenly over ½-cup portions of noodles. YIELD: 8 servings.

CALORIES 307; FAT 5.6g (sat 1.8g, mono 1.9g, poly 0.7g); PROTEIN 29.5g; CARB 30g; FIBER 3g; CHOL 91mg; IRON 4mg; SODIUM 252mg; CALC 32mg

Osso Buco

This recipe creates a succulent meal from inexpensive veal shanks by cooking them using a moist-heat method in a Dutch oven. A traditional Italian dish, osso buco is usually served with gremolata—a topping of minced parsley, lemon peel, and garlic.

4 (5-ounce) veal shanks
2 tablespoons all-purpose flour
Olive oil-flavored cooking spray
½ cup chopped onion
½ cup chopped carrot
2 (14½-ounce) cans no-salt-added diced tomatoes, undrained
½ cup dry white wine
½ cup canned fat-free, less-sodium beef broth
½ teaspoon salt
¼ teaspoon freshly ground pepper
1½ teaspoons minced fresh parsley (optional)
1½ teaspoons grated lemon rind (optional)
1½ teaspoons minced garlic (optional)

1. Trim fat from veal; dredge in flour. Coat a large Dutch oven with cooking spray; place over medium-high heat until hot. Add veal; cook until browned on all sides. Remove veal; set aside, and keep warm. Wipe drippings from Dutch oven.

2. Coat Dutch oven with cooking spray; place over medium-high heat until hot. Add onion and carrot; sauté until tender. Stir in tomato and next 4 ingredients; add veal. Bring to a boil; cover, reduce heat, and simmer 20 minutes. Uncover and simmer 30 minutes or until veal is tender. Spoon vegetable mixture over veal. If desired, sprinkle with parsley, lemon rind, and garlic.

YIELD: 4 servings.

CALORIES 189; FAT 2.7g (sat 0.7g, mono 0.9g, poly 0.3g); PROTEIN 20.3g; CARB 15.5g; FIBER 4g; CHOL 70mg; IRON 1.5mg; SODIUM 480mg; CALC 58mg

Cumin-Rubbed Pork Chops

4 (4-ounce) boneless center-cut loin pork chops	1 cup rinsed and drained canned black beans
2 teaspoons ground cumin	⅓ cup bottled thick and chunky salsa
¼ teaspoon salt	¼ cup chopped fresh cilantro or parsley
Cooking spray	
1 cup diced peeled mango or papaya	

1. Prepare grill. Sprinkle both sides of pork with cumin and salt; coat pork with cooking spray. Place pork on grill rack coated with cooking spray; grill, covered, 5 minutes on each side or until done. **2.** Combine mango, beans, and salsa in a small bowl. Serve mango mixture with pork chops; sprinkle with cilantro. **YIELD:** 4 servings.

CALORIES 273; FAT 11.5g (sat 4.1g, mono 5g, poly 0.9g); PROTEIN 27.4g; CARB 16.4g; FIBER 4g; CHOL 70mg; IRON 2mg; SODIUM 500mg; CALC 65mg

Peppercorn Pork Loin Roast

The memorable flavor of this tender pork roast comes from the Dijon mustard and the crispy coating of whole wheat breadcrumbs, peppercorns, and fresh thyme. Because of the peppercorn and fresh herbs, very little salt is needed.

1 (2½-pound) lean, boneless pork loin roast
3 tablespoons Dijon mustard
1 tablespoon nonfat buttermilk
2 cups soft whole wheat bread-crumbs
2 tablespoons cracked black pepper
2 teaspoons whole assorted peppercorns, crushed
2 teaspoons chopped fresh thyme
¼ teaspoon salt
Cooking spray
Fresh thyme sprigs (optional)

1. Preheat oven to 325°.

2. Trim fat from roast. Combine mustard and buttermilk. Spread mustard mixture over roast.

3. Combine breadcrumbs and next 4 ingredients; press bread-crumb mixture evenly onto roast. Place roast on a rack in a roast-ing pan coated with cooking spray. Insert a meat thermometer into thickest part of roast, if desired. Bake at 325° for 2 hours or until meat thermometer registers 160°. Let stand 10 minutes before slicing. Garnish with thyme sprigs, if desired. YIELD: 10 servings (serving size: 3 ounces).

CALORIES 226; FAT 7.7g (sat 2.7g, mono 3.2g, poly 0.6g); PROTEIN 24.7g; CARB 13.3g; FIBER 2g; CHOL 63mg; IRON 1.6mg; SODIUM 239mg; CALC 29mg

RECIPE BENEFIT: low-carb

How To Buy Pork

Here are three fresh cuts of pork that *Cooking Light* uses often and what we look for at the grocery store when making purchases.

PORK TENDERLOIN

Pork tenderloin comes from the sirloin (the back part of the loin). It is a narrow cylinder about 1 foot in length and about 3 inches in diameter. Usually, you'll see 1-pound packages or 2 (¾-pound) tenderloins packaged together. The tenderloin is the leanest and most tender cut of pork.

PORK LOIN

Pork loin is solid both on the bone and boneless, usually in 2- to 4-pound roasts, and it is also cut into chops. The meat is tender but lean, especially the short loin (in the lower back). The rib area, which has a little more fat, is more flavorful and is the pork equivalent of the standing rib roast of beef or a rack of lamb; this cut is often labeled "center-cut pork loin." When pork loin is sold boneless, it's hard to tell where the piece has come from, but a skilled butcher should be able to guide you.

PORK CHOPS

Chops come from the loin. They may be bone-in or boneless, and they are usually named for the section of the loin from which they're cut. Buy chops at least 1 to 1¼ inches thick; they tend to brown nicely without overcooking.

- Rib chops are from the rib area and include some back-rib bone.
- Loin chops are from the lower back and have a characteristic T-shaped bone; they include a lot of loin meat and a bit of tenderloin meat.
- Sirloin chops are from the area around the hip and often include a big chunk of hipbone.

Chicken and Dumplings

Spoonfuls of low-fat baking mix dough form the dumplings in this classic American dish.

- 1 cup chopped celery (about 3 stalks)
- 1 cup chopped onion (about 1)
- 1 cup chopped carrot (about 2)
- ½ teaspoon pepper
- ¼ teaspoon poultry seasoning
- 1 (32-ounce) carton fat-free, less-sodium chicken broth
- 1½ cups water
- 2 cups low-fat baking mix
- 1 teaspoon dried parsley flakes
- ¾ cup fat-free milk
- 3 cups shredded roasted chicken

1. Combine first 6 ingredients in a Dutch oven; bring to a boil. Cover, reduce heat to medium, and cook 5 minutes.

2. Combine baking mix and parsley flakes. Add milk, stirring with a fork just until dry ingredients are moist.

3. Return broth mixture to a boil. Drop dough by rounded tablespoonfuls into boiling broth; reduce heat to medium. Cover and cook 15 minutes.

4. Add chicken to broth mixture, stirring gently. YIELD: 6 servings.

CALORIES 305; FAT 5.2g (sat 1.2g, mono 0.9g, poly 0.6g); PROTEIN 27.2g; CARB 35.2g; FIBER 1.9g; CHOL 60mg; IRON 2.4mg; SODIUM 865mg; CALC 105mg

Cajun Fire Chicken

Steam quick-cooking rice in the microwave to serve with this saucy dish.

Cooking spray
2 teaspoons olive oil
4 (4-ounce) skinless, boneless chicken breast halves
1 green bell pepper, coarsely chopped
1 (14½-ounce) can stewed tomatoes, undrained and chopped
2 teaspoons hot sauce
⅓ cup chopped fresh cilantro, divided
½ teaspoon dried thyme
Additional hot sauce (optional)
Fresh thyme sprigs (optional)

1. Heat oil in a large nonstick skillet coated with cooking spray over medium-high heat. Add chicken, and cook 2 minutes on each side or until lightly browned. Add pepper, tomatoes, 2 teaspoons hot sauce, ¼ cup cilantro, and dried thyme. Bring to a boil; cover, reduce heat, and simmer 5 minutes. Uncover and simmer 10 minutes.

2. Stir remaining cilantro into tomato mixture. Serve with additional hot sauce, and garnish with thyme sprigs, if desired.

YIELD: 4 servings.

CALORIES 216; FAT 4.2g (sat 1.2g, mono 1.4g, poly 1g); PROTEIN 35.6g; CARB 7.9g; FIBER 1.7g; CHOL 94mg; IRON 3mg; SODIUM 325mg; CALC 58mg

RECIPE BENEFIT: low-carb

Crispy Cornmeal Chicken

For a quick and neat way to pound the chicken, place the chicken, one piece at a time, in a heavy-duty, zip-top plastic bag. Seal the bag, and pound the chicken. Use the same bag for each piece of chicken; then discard the bag.

4 (6-ounce) skinned, boned chicken breast halves
⅓ cup yellow cornmeal
1 teaspoon chili powder
¼ teaspoon garlic powder
¼ teaspoon salt
1 tablespoon all-purpose flour
2 egg whites, lightly beaten
2 teaspoons canola oil
½ cup salsa

1. Place chicken between 2 sheets of heavy-duty plastic wrap, and flatten to ½-inch thickness, using a meat mallet or rolling pin.
2. Combine cornmeal and next 3 ingredients in a small bowl. Sprinkle flour evenly over each chicken breast half; dip in egg whites, and dredge in cornmeal mixture.
3. Heat oil in a large nonstick skillet over medium heat. Add chicken, and cook 5 to 6 minutes on each side or until chicken is done. Serve with salsa. **YIELD:** 4 servings.

CALORIES 274; FAT 4.7g (sat 0.8g, mono 2g, poly 1.3g); PROTEIN 42.7g; CARB 13.2g; FIBER 1g; CHOL 99mg; IRON 1.9mg; SODIUM 496mg; CALC 30mg

RECIPE BENEFIT: low-carb

Turkey Quesadillas

½ teaspoon canola oil
¾ cup chopped green bell pepper (about 1 small)
½ cup chopped red onion (about 1 small)
1 teaspoon ground cumin
1 cup chopped cooked turkey breast
¾ cup drained no-salt-added diced tomatoes
½ cup minced fresh cilantro
½ teaspoon salt
⅛ teaspoon freshly ground black pepper
4 (8-inch) fat-free flour tortillas
⅓ cup (1.5 ounces) shredded reduced-fat white Cheddar cheese (such as Cabot)
Cooking spray

1. Heat oil in a large nonstick skillet over medium-high heat. Add chopped pepper and onion; sauté 3 minutes. Add cumin; sauté 1 minute. Add turkey and tomato; sauté 3 minutes. Stir in cilantro, salt, and black pepper.

2. Place about ½ cup turkey mixture on half of each tortilla. Sprinkle cheese evenly over turkey; fold tortillas in half. Coat a large nonstick skillet with cooking spray; place over medium-high heat until hot. Add 2 filled tortillas; cook 30 seconds on each side or until lightly browned. Set aside, and keep warm. Repeat procedure with remaining 2 tortillas. Cut each folded tortilla into 3 wedges. YIELD: 4 servings (serving size: 3 wedges).

CALORIES 230; FAT 4.2g (sat 1.3g, mono 0.4g, poly 1.3g); PROTEIN 19.1g; CARB 30.3g; FIBER 5g; CHOL 37mg; IRON 2.3mg; SODIUM 726mg; CALC 197mg

QUICK TIP: Using a pizza cutter is a quick way to cut your quesadillas and have them ready to eat in no time.

Satisfy Your Sweet Tooth

Easy Peach Ice Cream

If you prefer strawberry ice cream to peach, use a 1-pound package of frozen unsweetened strawberries instead of peaches and ¾ teaspoon vanilla extract instead of coconut extract.

1 (1-pound) package frozen peaches	½ cup thawed orange juice concentrate
1½ cups sliced ripe banana (about 2)	¼ cup "measures-like-sugar" calorie-free sweetener
1 cup vanilla low-fat, no sugar added ice cream	¾ teaspoon coconut extract or ½ teaspoon almond extract

1. Combine all ingredients in a food processor; process until smooth. Serve immediately, or freeze, covered, in an airtight freezer-safe container until ready to serve. YIELD: 9 servings (serving size: ½ cup).

CALORIES 120; FAT 1.2g (sat 0.6g, mono 0.3g, poly 0.2g); PROTEIN 1.5g; CARB 27.9g; FIBER 1.8g; CHOL 3.9mg; IRON 0.4mg; SODIUM 17mg; CALC 26mg

RECIPE BENEFITS: low-fat; low-sodium

Cantaloupe Sherbet

1 large ripe cantaloupe,
  peeled and finely chopped
  (about 5 cups)
⅓ cup granulated sugar substitute
  with aspartame (such as Equal)
2 tablespoons lemon juice

2 teaspoons unflavored gelatin
¼ cup cold water
1 cup vanilla fat-free yogurt
  sweetened with aspartame
Cantaloupe wedge (optional)

1. Combine cantaloupe, sugar substitute, and lemon juice in container of an electric blender or food processor; cover and process until smooth. Transfer mixture to a medium bowl.

2. Sprinkle gelatin over cold water in a small saucepan; let stand 1 minute. Cook over low heat, stirring until gelatin dissolves, about 4 minutes. Add to cantaloupe mixture, stirring well. Add yogurt, stirring until smooth.

3. Pour mixture into an 8-inch square pan; freeze until almost firm. Transfer mixture to a large bowl; beat at high speed of an electric mixer until fluffy. Spoon mixture back into pan; freeze until firm. Scoop into individual serving dishes to serve. Garnish each serving with a cantaloupe wedge, if desired. YIELD: 5 servings (serving size: 1 cup).

CALORIES 76; FAT 0g; PROTEIN 2.7g; CARB 16g; FIBER 0g; CHOL 1mg; IRON 0mg; SODIUM 27mg; CALC 55mg

RECIPE BENEFITS: low-fat; low-sodium

SELECTION TIP: Skip the thumping and shaking; when selecting fresh cantaloupe, look for sweet-smelling melons that have a thick netting and a golden (not green) undertone. The stem end should have a small indentation. A small crack is a sign of sweetness, but avoid fruit with mold. The blossom end (opposite the stem end) should be slightly soft.

GARNISH TIP: Top each shortcake with a dollop of whipped topping or one strawberry slice and a mint sprig. This won't add any calories or carbohydrate, and your family will appreciate your effort to make the dessert extra special.

Strawberry Shortcakes

2 cups strawberries, sliced
2 tablespoons "measures-like-sugar" calorie-free sweetener
2 tablespoons low-sugar strawberry spread
1¾ cups all-purpose flour
2 teaspoons baking powder
¼ teaspoon baking soda
¼ teaspoon salt
2 teaspoons "meausures-like-sugar" calorie-free sweetener
3 tablespoons light stick butter
¾ cup plain fat-free yogurt
Frozen fat-free whipped topping, thawed (optional)
Mint sprigs (optional)

1. Preheat oven to 425°.

2. Stir together first 3 ingredients. Set aside.

3. Spoon flour into dry measuring cups; level with a knife. Combine four, baking powder, and next 3 ingredients; cut in butter with a pastry blender or 2 knives until mixture resembles coarse meal. Add yogurt, stirring just until dry ingredients are moist. Turn dough out onto a floured surface; knead 4 times. Roll to a ½-inch thickness; cut into 6 rounds with a 3-inch cutter. Place on an ungreased baking sheet. Bake at 425° for 10 minutes. Remove from baking sheet; cool on a wire rack.

4. Cut each biscuit in half horizontally. Spoon strawberry mixture evenly over bottom halves of biscuits. Place tops of biscuits on strawberries, cut sides down. Top with whipped topping and mint, if desired. **YIELD:** 6 servings.

CALORIES 200; FAT 3.5g (sat 1.8g, mono 0.1g, poly 0.2g); PROTEIN 5.6g; CARB 37.1g; FIBER 2.1g; CHOL 8mg; IRON 2.1mg; SODIUM 342mg; CALC 184mg

Kitchen Equipment Checklist

Here is a list of the essential kitchen equipment that is necessary for making desserts. It's certainly not a complete list, but it's a good start for the basics.

ASSORTED BAKING PANS

☐ Baking sheet
☐ Jelly-roll, 15- x 10-inch
☐ Loaf
☐ Muffin
☐ Round cake, 8- and 9-inch
☐ Springform, 7-, 8-, and 9-inch
☐ Square, 8- and 9-inch
☐ 13 x 9-inch
☐ Tart (round, removable-bottom)
☐ Tube, 10-inch
☐ Wire rack

POTS AND PANS

☐ Dutch oven: 3- to 6-quart
☐ Heavy saucepans
   ☐ small (1$\frac{1}{2}$-quart)
   ☐ medium (2-quart)
   ☐ large (3-quart)
☐ Nonstick skillets
   ☐ 10-inch
   ☐ 12-inch
☐ Cast-iron skillet
☐ Roasting pan (for water bath)

ASSORTED GLASS DISHES

☐ Baking dishes, 11- x 7- and 13- x 9-inch
☐ Pie plate, 9- and 10-inch
☐ Custard cups
☐ Regular and individual soufflé dishes

UTENSILS

☐ Basting brush
☐ Biscuit cutter, 3-inch
☐ Can opener
☐ Colander, strainer, and sieve
☐ Cookie scoops
☐ Corkscrew
☐ Graters: box and handheld
☐ Handheld juicer
☐ Heatproof spatula
☐ Ice cream scoop
☐ Kitchen shears or scissors
☐ Measuring cups
   ☐ dry and liquid
☐ Measuring spoons
☐ Melon baller
☐ Metal icing spatula
☐ Pastry blender
☐ Potato masher
☐ Rolling pin
☐ Thermometers
   ☐ candy
   ☐ instant-read
   ☐ oven
☐ Vegetable peeler
☐ Whisk
☐ Wooden and slotted spoons

OTHER EQUIPMENT

- ☐ Blender
- ☐ Cutting boards
- ☐ Food processor
- ☐ Food scale
- ☐ Glass mixing bowls
- ☐ Handheld electric mixer
- ☐ Ice cream freezer
- ☐ Kitchen torch
- ☐ Pepper mill
- ☐ Stand mixer

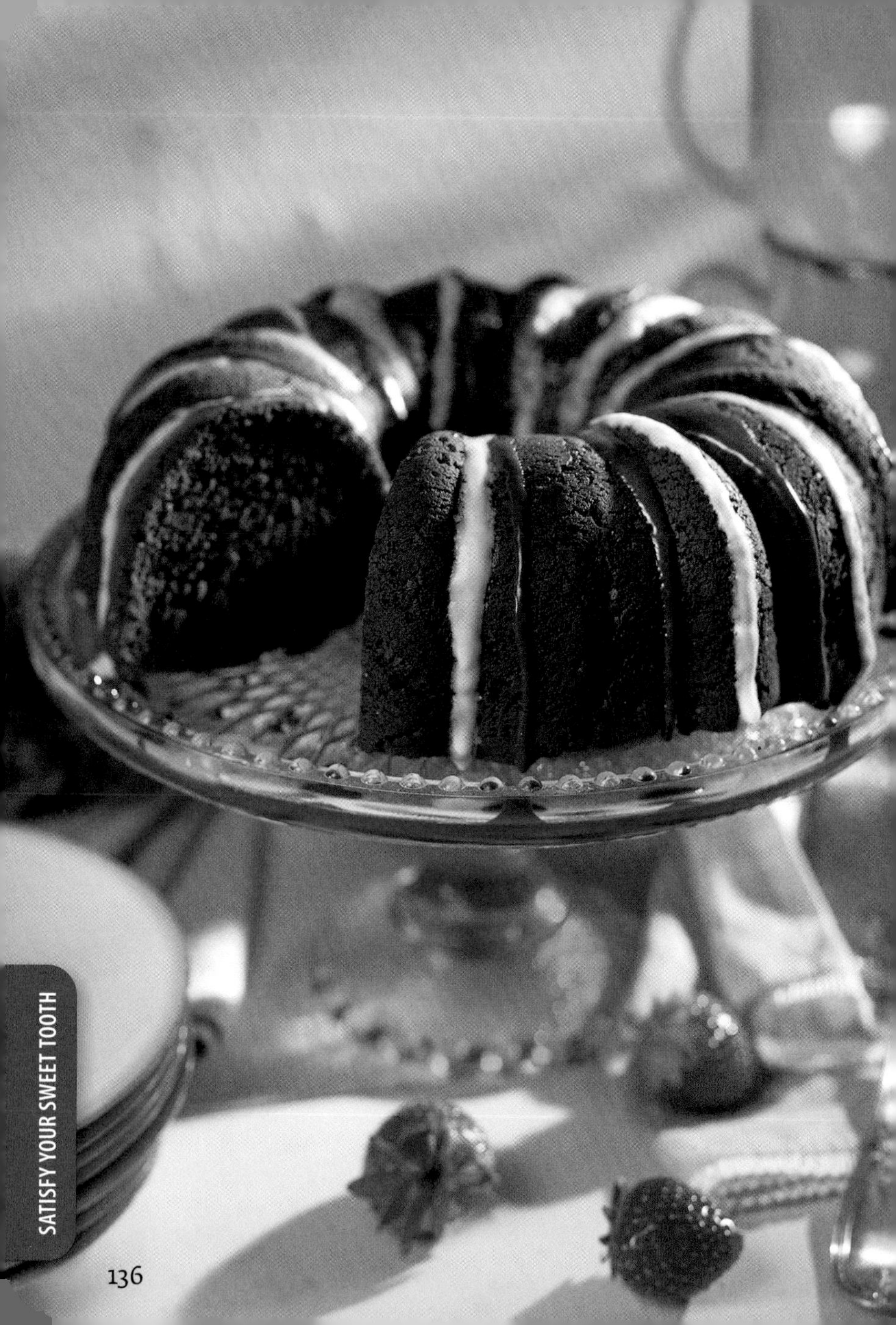

Triple-Chocolate Bundt Cake

½ cup unsweetened applesauce
1 (18.25-ounce) package moist devil's food cake mix
1 (1.4-ounce) package chocolate sugar-free pudding mix
1 cup fat-free sour cream
⅓ cup fat-free milk
3 large egg whites
1 large egg
1 teaspoon almond extract
Cooking spray
3 tablespoons Equal Measure
2½ teaspoons fat-free milk
1 ounce sugar-free milk chocolate
1 tablespoon fat-free milk

1. Spread applesauce onto several layers of paper towels. Cover with additional paper towels; let stand 5 minutes. Scrape into a bowl. Combine cake mix and next 6 ingredients in a large bowl; add applesauce. Beat with a mixer 2 minutes. Pour into a 12-cup Bundt pan coated with cooking spray. Bake at 350° for 53 minutes or until a pick inserted in center comes out clean. Cool in pan on wire rack 10 minutes; remove from pan. Cool completely on wire rack.
2. Combine sugar substitute and 2½ teaspoons milk; drizzle over cake. Place chocolate in a microwave-safe dish; microwave at HIGH 1½ minutes, stirring after 1 minute. Add 1 tablespoon milk; stir. Drizzle over cake. **YIELD:** 18 servings.

CALORIES 168; FAT 4.4g (sat 1.6g, mono 0.1g, poly 0g); PROTEIN 4.0g; CARB 28g; FIBER 0.7g; CHOL 31mg; IRON 1.1mg; SODIUM 286mg; CALC 66mg

New York Cheesecake

Crust:
- ⅔ cup all-purpose flour
- 3 tablespoons sugar
- 2 tablespoons chilled butter, cut into small pieces
- 1 tablespoon ice water
- Cooking spray

Filling:
- 4 cups fat-free cottage cheese
- 2 cups sugar
- 2 (8-ounce) blocks ⅓-less-fat cream cheese, softened
- ¼ cup all-purpose flour
- ½ cup fat-free sour cream
- 1 tablespoon grated lemon rind
- 1 tablespoon vanilla extract
- ¼ teaspoon salt
- 5 large eggs

1. Preheat oven to 400°.

2. To prepare crust, lightly spoon ⅔ cup flour into dry measuring cups; level with a knife. Place ⅔ cup flour and 3 tablespoons sugar in a food processor; pulse 2 times or until combined. Add butter; pulse 6 times or until mixture resembles coarse meal. With processor on, slowly pour ice water through food chute, processing just until blended (do not allow dough to form a ball).

3. Firmly press mixture into bottom of a 9 x 3-inch springform pan coated with cooking spray. Bake at 400° for 10 minutes or until lightly browned; cool on a wire rack.

4. Reduce oven temperature to 325°.

5. To prepare filling, strain cottage cheese through a cheesecloth-lined sieve 10 minutes; discard liquid. Place cottage cheese in food processor; process until smooth.

6. Place 2 cups sugar and cream cheese in a large bowl; beat with a mixer at medium speed until smooth. Lightly spoon ¼ cup flour into a dry measuring cup; level with a knife. Add ¼ cup flour, sour cream, and next 4 ingredients to cream cheese mixture;

beat well. Add cottage cheese, stirring until well blended. Pour cheese mixture into prepared crust.

7. Bake at 325° for 1½ hours or until almost set. Turn oven off. Cool cheesecake in closed oven 1 hour. Remove cheesecake from oven; run a knife around outside edge. Cool to room temperature. Cover and chill at least 8 hours. **YIELD:** 16 servings (serving size: 1 wedge). **NOTE:** You can also make cheesecake in a 10 x 2½-inch springform pan. Bake at 300° for 1½ hours or until almost set. Turn oven off. Cool cheesecake in closed oven 30 minutes.

CALORIES 291; FAT 9.8g (sat 5.7g, mono 3g, poly 0.5g); PROTEIN 12.9g; CARB 37.7g; FIBER 0.2g; CHOL 98mg; IRON 0.7mg; SODIUM 410mg; CALC 93mg

Banana Split Cake

1 (8-ounce) package white low-cal, sugar and sodium free cake mix
Cooking spray
1 (1.5-ounce) package sugar-free vanilla instant pudding mix
3 cups fat-free milk
1 (20-ounce) can no sugar added cherry pie filling
1 (15-ounce) can pineapple tidbits in juice, drained

1 (16-ounce) package frozen unsweetened whole strawberries, thawed and sliced
3 large ripe bananas, sliced
1 (16-ounce) container frozen light whipped topping, thawed
¾ cup chopped walnuts
¼ cup sugar-free chocolate syrup

1. Preheat oven to 350°.

2. Prepare cake mix according to package directions. Pour batter into a 13 x 9-inch baking pan coated with cooking spray. Bake at 350° for 12 minutes; cool slightly.

3. Prepare pudding according to package directions using 3 cups fat-free milk. Spread pudding over cake. Top with pie filling, pineapple, strawberries, and bananas. Top fruit with whipped topping. Sprinkle with walnuts, and drizzle with chocolate syrup. **YIELD:** 18 servings (serving size: 2 x 3-inch piece).

CALORIES 215; FAT 7.2g (sat 3.3g, mono 0.9g, poly 2.7g); PROTEIN 3.2g; CARB 36.9g; FIBER 2.1g; CHOL 0.5mg; IRON 0.9mg; SODIUM 108mg; CALC 57mg

RECIPE BENEFIT: low-sodium

NUTRITION TIP: A small banana has more than 2 grams of fiber; that's more fiber than a bowl of cornflakes or a dish of fresh blueberries.

Chocolate Peppermint Cookies

½ cup butter, softened
⅓ cup sugar
½ cup "measures-like-sugar" brown sugar calorie-free sweetener (such as Brown Sugar Twin)
½ cup egg substitute
1 teaspoon vanilla extract
2¼ cups all-purpose flour
1 teaspoon baking powder
¾ teaspoon baking soda
¼ teaspoon salt
⅓ cup unsweetened cocoa
⅔ cup finely crushed peppermint candies (about 30 candies)
Cooking spray

1. Preheat oven to 350°.

2. Beat butter with a mixer at medium speed until creamy; gradually add sugar and sweetener, beating well. Add egg substitute and vanilla; beat well.

3. Combine flour and next 4 ingredients. Add to margarine mixture, stirring just until blended. Stir in crushed candy. Drop dough by level tablespoonfuls onto wax paper. Roll into balls; place balls, 2 inches apart, on baking sheets coated with cooking spray. Flatten balls with a fork. Bake at 350° for 10 to 12 minutes. Remove from pans, and let cool on wire racks. YIELD: 38 servings (serving size: 1 cookie).

CALORIES 76; FAT 2.7g (sat 1.6g, mono 0.7g, poly 0.2g); PROTEIN 1.3g; CARB 11.9g; FIBER 0.5g; CHOL 6mg; IRON 0.5mg; SODIUM 76mg; CALC 16mg

RECIPE BENEFITS: low-fat; low-sodium; low-carb

Peanut Butter-and-Jelly Sandwich Cookies

¼ cup butter, softened
¼ cup creamy peanut butter, unsalted
½ cup granulated sugar substitute (such as Splenda)
¼ cup sugar
2 egg whites
1 teaspoon vanilla extract
1¾ cups all-purpose flour
1 teaspoon baking soda
⅛ teaspoon salt
Cooking spray
¾ cup strawberry fruit spread

1. Beat butter and peanut butter at medium speed of a mixer until creamy. Gradually add sugar substitute and sugar, beating well. Add egg whites and vanilla; beat well. Combine flour, soda, and salt in a small bowl, stirring well. Gradually add flour mixture to creamed mixture, mixing well.

2. Shape dough into 40 (1-inch) balls. Place balls 2 inches apart on cookie sheets coated with cooking spray. Flatten cookies into 2-inch circles using a flat-bottomed glass. Bake at 350° for 8 minutes or until lightly browned. Cool slightly on cookie sheets; remove from cookie sheets, and let cool completely on wire racks.

3. Spread about 1½ teaspoons strawberry spread on the bottom of half the cooled cookies; top with remaining cookies. **YIELD:** 20 sandwich cookies (serving size: 1 cookie).

CALORIES 115; FAT 4.0g (sat 1.8g, mono 1.4g, poly 0.6g); PROTEIN 2.3g; CARB 17.5g; FIBER 0.5g; CHOL 6mg; IRON 0.6mg; SODIUM 100mg; CALC 4mg

RECIPE BENEFITS: low-sodium

Tips for Great Low-Fat Cookies

Here are our Test Kitchen professionals' tips for making cookies that melt in your mouth:

1. Measure flour correctly; too much flour will make the cookies tough (see page 159 for how to measure).

2. If the batter seems dry, don't give in to the temptation to add more liquid. This makes for a cakelike cookie that spreads too much.

3. Use the exact ingredients called for in the recipe. Baking cookies is like conducting a science experiment, because both the right balance and type of ingredients are crucial.

4. Cookies bake more evenly when they're about the same size. And don't forget that they need plenty of space between them to allow for spreading.

5. We bake cookies on the second rack from the bottom of the oven. Be sure there is room left for air to circulate on all sides after the baking sheet is placed on the rack.

Angel Food Puffs

½ cup orange-flavored sugar-free carbonated beverage
¼ teaspoon almond extract

1 (16-ounce) package angel food cake mix
Cooking spray

1. Preheat oven to 350°.

2. Combine first 3 ingredients in a large bowl. Beat with a mixer at medium speed until smooth. Drop batter by heaping tablespoons onto baking sheets coated with cooking spray.

3. Bake at 350° for 9 minutes or until lightly browned. Remove from baking sheets immediately, and cool on wire racks. YIELD: 28 cookies (serving size: 1 cookie).

CALORIES 59; FAT 0g; PROTEIN 1.5g; CARB 13.2g; FIBER 0g; CHOL 0mg; IRON 0mg; SODIUM 98mg; CALC 9mg

RECIPE BENEFITS: low-fat; low-sodium; low-carb

You can change the flavor of these light, chewy cookies by using any other flavored sugar-free carbonated beverage. Try strawberry or lemon-lime for starters.

CHOICE INGREDIENT: *Cocoa powder*

Cocoa powder is made from ground roasted cacao seeds. It is the best choice for light baking, because it delivers the richest chocolaty flavor with the least amount of fat. There are two types: natural (nonalkalized) and Dutch process (alkalized). Though both are unsweetened cocoa, their flavors differ slightly. Natural cocoa is tart and acidic, while Dutch process cocoa has a mellow toasted flavor. It's best to store cocoa in an airtight container away from herbs, spices, and other aromatic substances. It picks up other flavors easily.

Fudgy Cream Cheese Brownies

Don't use reduced-calorie or fat-free tub margarine in this recipe because those products contain water, which will make the brownies gummy.

¾ cup sugar
¼ cup plus 2 tablespoons light stick butter, softened
1 large egg
1 large egg white
1 tablespoon vanilla extract
½ cup all-purpose flour

¼ cup unsweetened cocoa
Cooking spray
1 (8-ounce) block ⅓-less-fat cream cheese, softened
¼ cup "measures-like-sugar" calorie-free sweetener
3 tablespoons 1% low-fat milk

1. Preheat oven to 350°.

2. Beat sugar and butter with a mixer at medium speed until light and fluffy. Add egg, egg white, and vanilla; beat well. Gradually add flour and cocoa, beating well. Pour into an 8-inch square pan coated with cooking spray.

3. Beat cream cheese and sweetener with a mixer at high speed until smooth. Add milk; beat well. Pour cream cheese mixture over chocolate mixture; swirl together using the tip of a knife to create a marbled effect.

4. Bake at 350° for 30 minutes. Cool completely in pan on a wire rack. Cut into squares. YIELD: 16 servings (serving size: 1 square).

CALORIES 123; FAT 6.2g (sat 3.9g, mono 0.9g, poly 0.2g); PROTEIN 3.1g; CARB 13.9g; FIBER 0.6g; CHOL 27mg; IRON 0.5mg; SODIUM 95mg; CALC 20mg

RECIPE BENEFITS: low-sodium; low-carb

A SPRINGFORM PAN—a round, deep pan with tall, removable sides—is the most commonly used pan for baking cheesecakes. But we've also chosen to use it for our Chocolate-Macadamia Nut Pie. Although it may be an unconventional method, it works beautifully in this particular application. Simply remove the sides of the springform pan, let stand 10 minutes, garnish, and serve!

Chocolate-Macadamia Nut Pie

1⅔ cups crushed sugar-free
    chocolate sandwich cookies
3 tablespoons butter
Cooking spray
2 cups chocolate sugar-free ice
    cream, softened
1 (3½-ounce) jar macadamia nuts,
    coarsely chopped

2 (8-ounce) containers fat-free
    frozen whipped topping, thawed
Shaved sugar-free chocolate bars
    (optional)
Toasted macadamia nuts (optional)
Whipped topping (optional)

1. Combine crushed cookies and butter. Press mixture firmly in bottom of a 9-inch springform pan coated with cooking spray.
2. Combine softened ice cream and nuts, stirring well. Fold in whipped topping. Pour mixture into prepared crust.
3. Cover and freeze until firm.
4. To serve, remove sides of springform pan, let stand 10 minutes before serving. Garnish with chocolate shavings, toasted nuts, and whipped topping, if desired (chocolate, nuts, and whipped topping not included in analysis). **YIELD:** 10 servings (serving size: 1 wedge).

CALORIES 277; FAT 15.4g (sat 4.2g, mono 6.8g, poly 0.3g); PROTEIN 2.9g; CARB 26g; FIBER 2.4g; CHOL 9mg; IRON 0.7mg; SODIUM 121mg; CALC 5mg

RECIPE BENEFIT: low-sodium

Deep-Dish Cherry Pie

1½ cups all-purpose flour
1½ tablespoons "measures-like-sugar" calorie-free sweetener
¼ teaspoon salt
6 tablespoons vegetable shortening
6 tablespoons ice water
¾ teaspoon cider vinegar

4 (16-ounce) cans tart cherries in water
½ cup "measures-like-sugar" calorie-free sweetener
⅓ cup cornstarch
1 teaspoon ground cinnamon
½ teaspoon almond extract

1. Preheat oven to 400°.

2. Combine flour, 1½ tablespoons sweetener, and salt. Cut in shortening until mixture resembles coarse meal. Add ice water and vinegar; toss with a fork until moist. Shape into a ball. Roll into a 14-inch circle on a lightly floured surface. Place dough in a 10-inch pieplate; press against bottom and sides of plate. Flute edges.

3. Drain cherries, reserving 1¼ cups liquid. Set cherries aside. Combine reserved cherry liquid, ½ cup sweetener, and cornstarch in a saucepan; stir well. Cook over medium heat until very thick, stirring constantly. Stir in cherries, cinnamon, and almond extract.

4. Pour mixture into pastry shell. Shield pastry with foil, and bake at 400° for 20 minutes. Reduce heat to 375°; bake, unshielded, 25 to 30 minutes or until hot and bubbly. Serve warm or at room temperature. **YIELD:** 10 servings (serving size: 1 wedge).

CALORIES 219; FAT 8.0g (sat 2.0g, mono 3.2g, poly 2.3g); PROTEIN 3.4g; CARB 34.6g; FIBER 2.7g; CHOL 0mg; IRON 3.5mg; SODIUM 72mg; CALC 26mg

RECIPE BENEFIT: low-sodium

CHOICE INGREDIENT: *Cherries*

Cherries open the stone fruit season in late May. Dark red Bing cherries are the popular American standard, but yellow Queen Annes, white and red Rainiers, and sour Montmorencys are widely available. Smaller and more rounded in shape, sour (or tart) cherries are usually used for pies. Most sour cherries are canned, frozen, or dried, or used to make juice. Cherries do not ripen after harvest, so once picked, their sweetness is set. Store fresh cherries for up to a week in the refrigerator in a bowl lined with paper towels.

You'll love the cool creaminess of this frozen pie with the contrasting crunch of the oven-toasted rice cereal. It's a true treat any time of the year.

Crispy Peanut Butterscotch Pie

¼ cup creamy peanut butter
1 tablespoon honey
1½ cups oven-toasted rice cereal (such as Rice Krispies)
1 (1-ounce) package sugar-free butterscotch instant pudding mix
2 cups fat-free milk
1½ cups frozen fat-free whipped topping, thawed and divided
Ground cinnamon (optional)
Additional oven-toasted rice cereal (optional)

1. Combine peanut butter and honey in a medium microwave-safe bowl; microwave at HIGH 30 seconds, stirring until mixture melts. Stir in rice cereal. Using wax paper, press cereal mixture into bottom of an 8-inch round cake pan.
2. Prepare pudding mix according to package directions, using 2 cups fat-free milk; fold in 1 cup whipped topping. Spoon pudding mixture into prepared pan. Cover and freeze until firm. Let pie stand at room temperature 15 minutes before serving.
3. Cut pie into 6 wedges, and top evenly with remaining whipped topping. If desired, sprinkle with ground cinnamon and additional cereal. **YIELD:** 6 servings.

CALORIES 175; FAT 5.5g (sat 1.1g, mono 2.6g, poly 1.5g); PROTEIN 6.1g; CARB 22.8g; FIBER 0.7g; CHOL 1mg; IRON 0.6mg; SODIUM 257mg; CALC 88mg

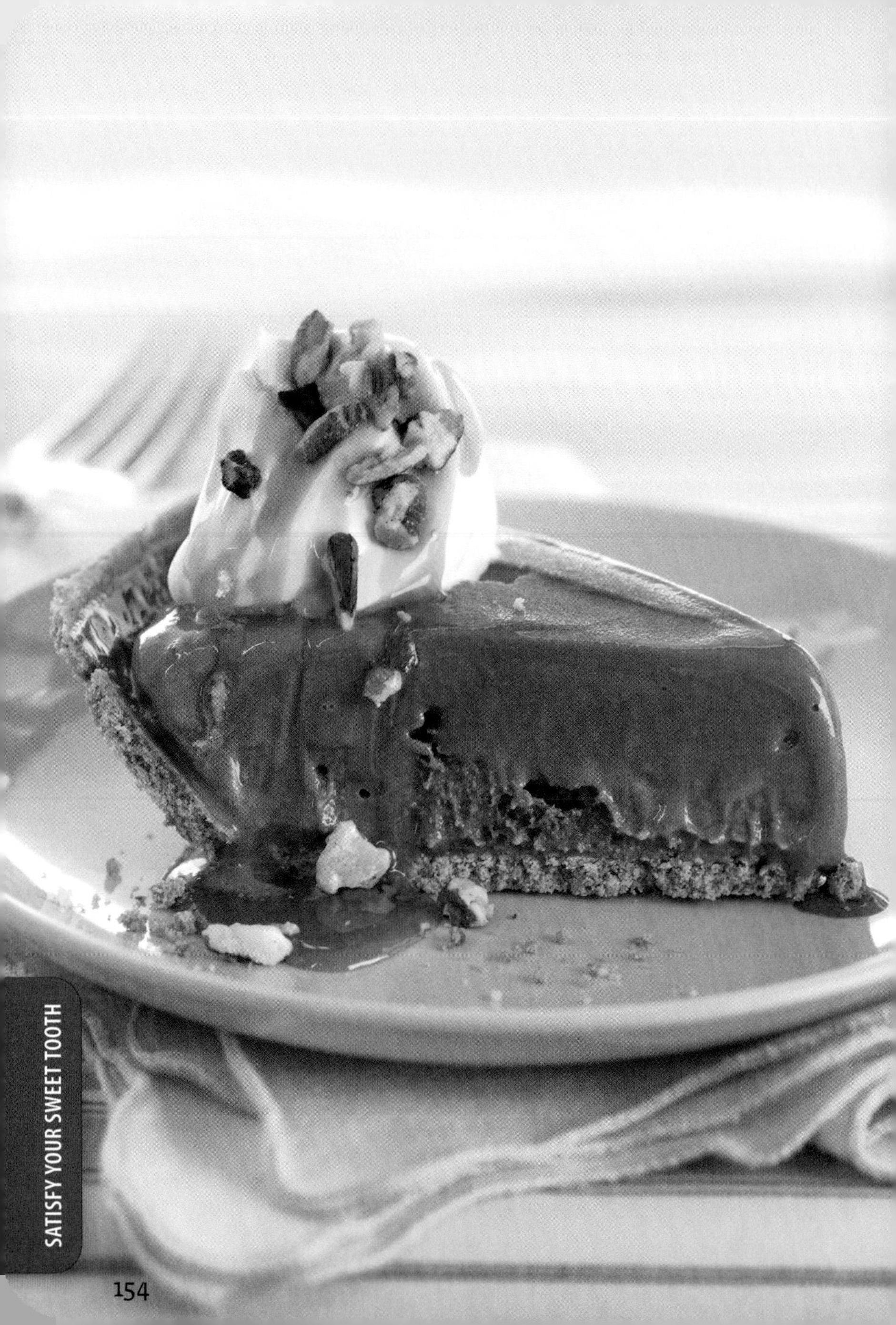

Turtle Pie

4 cups chocolate sugar-free ice cream, softened

$\frac{1}{2}$ cup fat-free caramel topping, divided

1 (6-ounce) reduced-fat graham cracker crust

$\frac{2}{3}$ cup frozen fat-free whipped topping, thawed

2 tablespoons chopped pecans, toasted

1. Place an extra-large bowl in freezer for at least 5 minutes. Spoon ice cream into chilled bowl; stir in $\frac{1}{4}$ cup caramel topping. Spoon ice cream mixture into pie crust; cover and freeze $2\frac{1}{2}$ hours or until firm.

2. Place pie in refrigerator to soften 10 to 15 minutes before serving.

3. Heat $\frac{1}{4}$ cup caramel topping according to label directions. Cut pie into 10 wedges, and top evenly with whipped topping. Drizzle evenly with warm caramel topping, and sprinkle with pecans.

YIELD: 10 servings (serving size: 1 slice).

CALORIES 214; FAT 6.3g (sat 0.5g, mono 0.6g, poly 0.3g); PROTEIN 3.3g; CARB 35.3g; FIBER 2.5g; CHOL 0mg; IRON 0.3mg; SODIUM 150mg; CALC 1mg

RECIPE BENEFIT: low-sodium

> **QUICK TIP:** If you don't have time to toast your pecans in the oven try the microwave quick method. Place the nuts in a shallow microwave-safe dish. Microwave at HIGH 1 to 3 minutes, stirring every 30 seconds. The nuts won't turn golden, but they'll have a toasted flavor.

Lemon Meringue Pie

We used fructose in the meringue, because it browns better than other sugar replacements.

½ (15-ounce) package refrigerated piecrusts
1 (0.3-ounce) package lemon sugar-free gelatin
1 cup boiling water
½ cup cold water
3 egg yolks, lightly beaten
3 tablespoons cornstarch

3 tablespoons fresh lemon juice
6 packets calorie-free sweetener with aspartame (such as Equal packets)
3 egg whites
¼ teaspoon cream of tartar
3 tablespoons granulated fructose

1. Preheat oven to 450°.

2. Bake 1 piecrust in a 9-inch pieplate according to package directions. Set aside. Reduce oven temperature to 350°.

3. Combine gelatin and boiling water in a saucepan, stirring until gelatin dissolves. Stir in cold water; let stand 10 minutes.

4. Add egg yolks, cornstarch, and lemon juice; stir. Place over medium heat; cook, stirring constantly, until mixture comes to a boil. Boil 1 minute. Remove from heat; stir in sweetener. Pour into crust.

5. Beat egg whites and cream of tartar with a mixer at high speed until foamy. Add fructose; beat until stiff peaks form. Spoon meringue smoothly over filling. Bake at 350° on lower rack in oven for 12 minutes. Cool on a wire rack; chill. **YIELD:** 8 servings (serving size: 1 wedge).

CALORIES 182; FAT 8.9g (sat 3.2g, mono 0.8g, poly 0.3g); PROTEIN 3.1g; CARB 21.6g; FIBER 0.1g; CHOL 97mg; IRON 0.2mg; SODIUM 133mg; CALC 11mg

RECIPE BENEFIT: low-sodium

How To Keep Meringue from Shrinking

Q: How do you keep meringue from shrinking on pies?

A: Cover the entire pie—all the way to the crust edges—with the meringue. This step seals the meringue to the pie, preventing it from pulling away and shrinking.

Measure Ingredients for Stellar Desserts

Measuring ingredients when preparing desserts is very important. It can mean the difference between a prize-winning delight and a disappointing disaster.

Creating healthy, scrumptious desserts depends on adding just the right amount of ingredients. Get in the habit of measuring with precision. Liquid and dry ingredients are measured using different techniques and utensils.

Liquid Ingredients

When measuring liquid ingredients, always use a liquid measuring cup so you can see the exact measurement through the side of the cup. If you measure liquid ingredients in a dry measuring cup, you may add too much or too little liquid. After you pour in the liquid, check the amount at eye level. Or use a liquid measuring cup with an angled surface that allows you to look down into the cup and read the measurement correctly.

No-Stick Measuring

If you're measuring honey, molasses, or peanut butter for a recipe that also includes oil, measure the oil first. The oil will coat the inside so that the sweetener won't stick to the cup. Or coat the inside of a measuring cup with cooking spray first before measuring the sticky ingredient.

Dry Ingredients

In general, healthy recipes call for less fat than traditional recipes. When fat is reduced in baking, the precise measurement of flour becomes crucial. Too much flour results in a very dry product. How you measure flour can make a huge difference—as much as an ounce per cup. If flour is scooped out of the canister with the measuring cup, it's likely that too much flour will be used. Therefore, correctly measuring flour is extremely important when making light recipes. Specific directions for measuring flour are included with recipes that call for $1/4$ cup or more of flour.

How To Measure Flour

1. Rather than scooping the flour out of the canister or bag, fluff the flour with a fork. Then lightly spoon the flour into a dry measuring cup without compacting it. Scooping the flour can add up to $3^1/2$ tablespoons per cup too much flour.

2. Level the top of the flour with a knife or a straight edge to get an even cup, scraping excess back into the canister.

Chocolate-Hazelnut Mousse Cups

2 (12.3-ounce) packages reduced-fat firm silken tofu (such as Mori-Nu Lite)
½ cup sugar
6 tablespoons unsweetened cocoa
2 tablespoons Frangelico (hazelnut-flavored liqueur)
½ teaspoon vanilla extract
Dash of salt
⅓ cup dark chocolate chips (such as Hershey's Special Dark)
18 chocolate graham crackers (4½ cookie sheets)
9 tablespoons frozen fat-free whipped topping, thawed
3 tablespoons chopped hazelnuts, toasted

1. Place first 6 ingredients in a food processor; process 20 seconds or until smooth.

2. Place chocolate chips in a small microwave-safe bowl. Microwave at HIGH 1 minute; stir until smooth. Add chocolate to tofu mixture; process until smooth. Transfer mousse to a bowl; cover and chill at least two hours.

3. Spoon about ⅓ cup mousse into each of 9 small individual dessert dishes. Coarsely crush 2 graham crackers over each mousse cup. Top each mousse cup with 1 tablespoon fat-free whipped topping, and sprinkle with 1 teaspoon hazelnuts. **YIELD:** 9 servings (serving size: 1 mousse cup).

CALORIES 179; FAT 5.3g (sat 2.3g, mono 1.4g, poly 0.4g); PROTEIN 6.1g; CARB 27.4g; FIBER 2.1g; CHOL 0mg; IRON 1.7mg; SODIUM 71mg; CALC 26mg

RECIPE BENEFIT: low-sodium

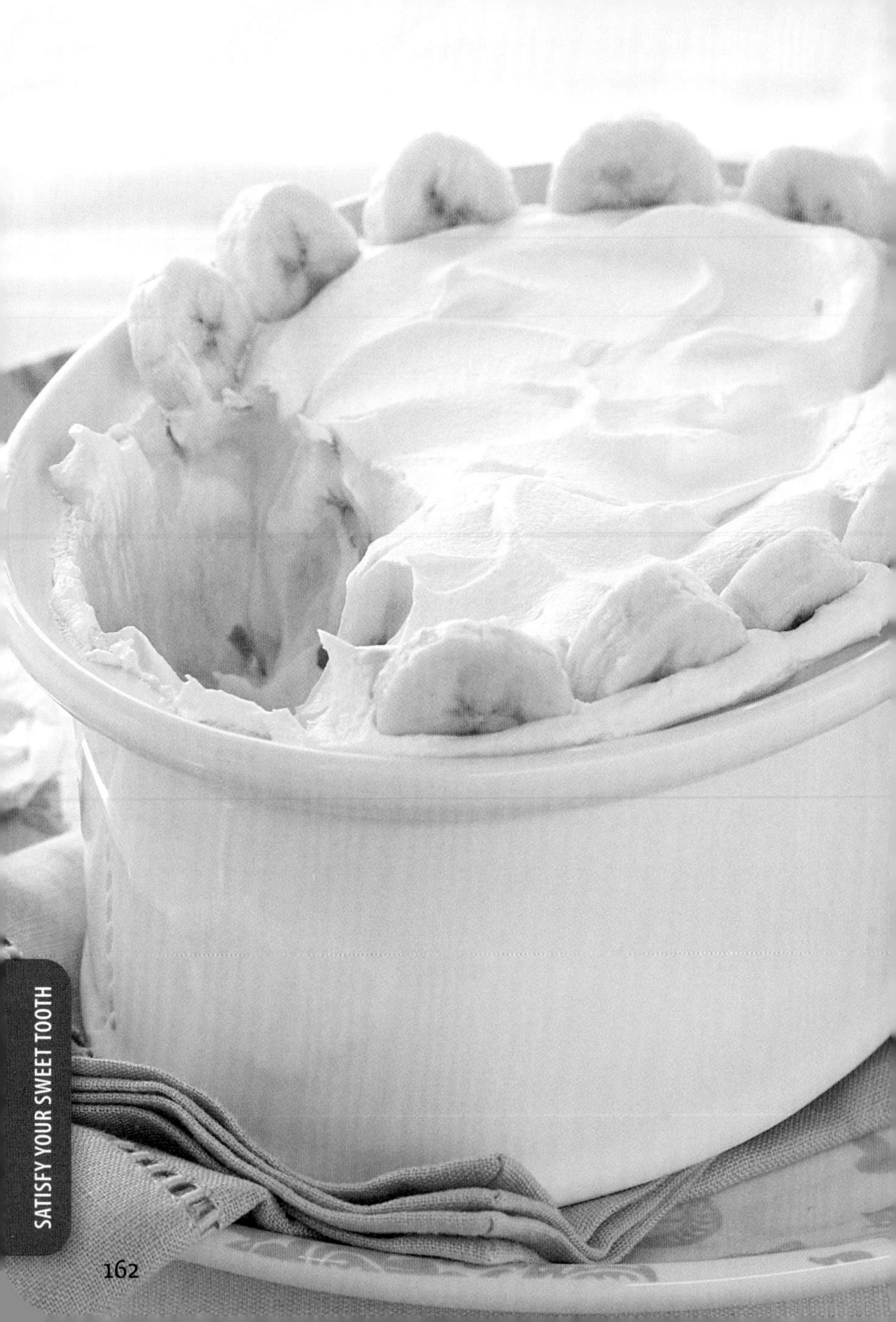

Peanut Butter-Banana Pudding

1 (1-ounce) package vanilla sugar-free, fat-free instant pudding mix

2 cups fat-free milk

⅓ cup creamy peanut butter, unsalted

1 (8-ounce) carton fat-free sour cream

42 reduced-fat vanilla wafers, divided

6 small bananas, divided

1 (8-ounce) carton frozen fat-free whipped topping, thawed

1 tablespoon lemon juice

1. Prepare pudding mix according to package directions, using a whisk and 2 cups fat-free milk. (Do not use an electric mixer.) Add peanut butter and sour cream, stirring well with a wire whisk.

2. Line bottom of a 2½-quart casserole with 14 vanilla wafers. Peel and slice 4 bananas. Top wafers with one-third each of pudding mixture, banana slices, and whipped topping. Repeat layers twice using remaining wafers, pudding mixture, banana, and topping. Cover and chill at least 2 hours. Peel and slice remaining 2 bananas; toss with lemon juice. Arrange slices around outer edges of dish. **YIELD:** 12 servings (serving size: about 1 cup).

CALORIES 202; FAT 4.6g (sat 0.8g, mono 1.7g, poly 1.0g); PROTEIN 4.8g; CARB 33.1g; FIBER 1.5g; CHOL 2.2mg; IRON 0.6mg; SODIUM 155mg; CALC 70mg

INGREDIENT TIP: Tossing the bananas with lemon juice is more about preserving color and texture rather than enhancing flavor. When coated with lemon juice, the bananas will keep from turning brown so quickly.

Double-Chocolate Pudding Parfaits

1 (1-ounce) package
white chocolate sugar-free,
fat-free instant pudding mix
2 cups fat-free milk

4 sugar-free soft Rocky Road
cookies, crumbled (such as
Archway)

1. Prepare pudding mix according to package directions, using 2 cups fat-free milk; cover and chill.

2. Place 2 tablespoons crumbled cookies in each of 4 parfait glasses; top each with ½ cup pudding. Top evenly with remaining crumbled cookies, and serve. YIELD: 4 servings (serving size: 1 parfait).

CALORIES 179; FAT 4.9g (sat 1.2g, mono 1.7g, poly 1.0g); PROTEIN 6.6g; CARB 27.1g; FIBER 1.3g; CHOL 1.5mg; IRON 0.8mg; SODIUM 326mg; CALC 167mg

Tiramisù

2 cups ½-inch cubed fat-free pound cake (about 5 ounces)

1 (0.44-ounce) envelope sugar-free mocha-flavored cappuccino mix

2 cups 1% low-fat milk, divided

1 (8-ounce) package fat-free cream cheese, softened

1 (1-ounce) package vanilla sugar-free, fat-free instant pudding mix

1 (0.43-ounce) envelope sugar-free vanilla-flavored cappuccino mix

2 cups fat-free frozen whipped topping, thawed

Grated sugar-free milk chocolate bar (optional)

1. Place ¼ cup cake cubes into each of 8 glasses. Combine mocha-flavored cappuccino mix with ½ cup milk; drizzle mixture evenly over cake in each glass.

2. Beat cream cheese with a mixer at medium speed just until smooth. Add remaining 1½ cups milk; beat until smooth. Add pudding mix and vanilla-flavored cappuccino mix; beat at low speed until blended. Fold whipped topping into pudding mixture. Spoon mixture evenly over cake. Garnish with grated sugar-free chocolate, if desired (grated chocolate not included in analysis). Cover and chill at least 3 hours. **YIELD:** 8 servings (serving size: 1 cup).

CALORIES 150; FAT 1.3g (sat 0.7g, mono 0.3g, poly 0.1g); PROTEIN 7.1g; CARB 23.5g; FIBER 0.3g; CHOL 4.7mg; IRON 0.5mg; SODIUM 332mg; CALC 136mg

RECIPE BENEFIT: low-fat

Nutritional Analysis

How to Use It and Why Glance at the end of any *Cooking Light* recipe, and you'll see how committed we are to helping you make the best of today's light cooking. With chefs, registered dietitians, home economists, and a computer system that analyzes every ingredient, *Cooking Light* gives you authoritative dietary detail like no other magazine. We go to such lengths so you can see how our recipes fit into your healthful eating plan. If you're trying to lose weight, the calorie and fat figures will probably help most. But if you're keeping a close eye on the sodium, cholesterol, and saturated fat in your diet, we provide those numbers, too. And because many women don't get enough iron or calcium, we can also help there, as well. Finally, there's a fiber analysis for those of us who don't get enough roughage.

Here's a helpful guide to put our nutritional analysis numbers into perspective. Remember, one size doesn't fit all, so take your lifestyle, age, and circumstances into consideration when determining your nutrition needs. For example, pregnant or breast-feeding women need more protein, calories, and calcium. And men older than 50 need 1,200mg of calcium daily, 200mg more than the amount recommended for younger men.

In Our Nutritional Analysis, We Use These Abbreviations

sat	saturated fat	**CHOL**	cholesterol
mono	monounsaturated fat	**CALC**	calcium
poly	polyunsaturated fat	**g**	gram
CARB	carbohydrates	**mg**	milligram

Daily Nutrition Guide

	Women Ages 25 to 50	Women over 50	Men over 24
Calories	2,000	2,000 or less	2,700
Protein	50g	50g or less	63g
Fat	65g or less	65g or less	88g or less
Saturated Fat	20g or less	20g or less	27g or less
Carbohydrates	304g	304g	410g
Fiber	25g to 35g	25g to 35g	25g to 35g
Cholesterol	300mg or less	300mg or less	300mg or less
Iron	18mg	8mg	8mg
Sodium	2,300mg or less	1,500mg or less	2,300mg or less
Calcium	1,000mg	1,200mg	1,000mg